UNOFFICIAL

MINECRAFT
LAB FOR KIDS

Family-Friendly Projects for Exploring
and Teaching Math, Science, History,
and Culture through Creative Building

JOHN MILLER
AND
CHRIS FORNELL SCOTT

QUARRY

Quarto is the authority on a wide range of topics.

Quarto educates, entertains and enriches the lives of our readers—enthusiasts and lovers of hands-on living.

www.QuartoKnows.com

First published in the United States of America in 2016 by
Quarry Books, an imprint of
Quarto Publishing Group USA Inc.
100 Cummings Center
Suite 406-L
Beverly, Massachusetts 01915-6101
Telephone: (978) 282-9590
Fax: (978) 283-2742
QuartoKnows.com
Visit our blogs at QuartoKnows.com

10 9 8 7 6 5

ISBN: 978-1-63159-117-4
Digital edition published in 2016
eISBN: 978-1-59253-185-3
Library of Congress Cataloging-in-Publication Data Available

Cover and Book Design: Kathie Alexander
Photography: Glenn Scott Photography on page 7, 8, 10, 11, 12, 16, 18, 21, 79 (bottom), 83 (bottom right), 87 (bottom), 109, 115, 130, 131; Shutterstock.com, page 25, 43, 51, 55, 60, 61, 62 (middle left) GTS Productions, 65, 73, 91 RitchardD, 101 (top right) biblphoto, 119, 127 (bottom), 137, 139

NOT AN OFFICIAL MINECRAFT PRODUCT. NOT APPROVED BY OR ASSOCIATED WITH MOJANG.

Printed in China

To my wife Audrey, for believing in me.

— JM

To the child in all of us who isn't afraid of
where new adventures might lead. To my sons,
Josiah, Eli, and Finn. You inspire me.

— CFS

Contents

BONUS: STICKER BADGES

Introduction

In an age where games have multimillion-dollar budgets, high-end computer graphics, and Hollywood-inspired storylines, how can a game that comes with no instructions, no clear goals, and no-frills blocky graphics become a mega-hit widely lauded for its creative and immersive play?

Perhaps it's because players walk away from a Minecraft session with a deep sense of fulfillment and are highly motivated to return and improve their skills. Minecraft challenges them to explore a new, unlimited world and interact with other players and the environment. They mine for resources and craft tools that they use to modify their environment to fit their needs. Or perhaps it's because Minecraft is versatile and highly adaptable to any player at any experience level and has something to teach everyone. Its open-ended nature provides rich opportunities for exploration and discovery and satisfies a natural inquisitiveness while promoting detailed and deep conversations, both in and out of the game.

Adults might assume that playing Minecraft is just like playing any other video game, but kids know that Minecraft offers much more than entertainment. As kids become experts in Minecraft, they create a knowledge gap that is often difficult for adults to bridge. Players can speak the language of Minecraft while nonplayers may be confused.

This book bridges that gap. It's designed for adults who want to connect with their Minecraft players by improving their understanding of the game and by extending their child's learning with both in- and out-of-game activities. It employs analog (community) connections that encourage kids to interact with the adults in their lives. New conversations and paths of creativity will reveal themselves as you complete both the in-game and out-of-game portions of the individual labs and the quests (a set of four labs). In some instances, you'll help the Minecraft expert with the analog connections, and at other times, the game expert will teach you how to build in-game portions of the lab.

WHAT CAN MINECRAFT TEACH?

You only need to peek just beneath the surface of Minecraft to uncover rich and varied learning experiences. Minecraft encourages players to create, share, and innovate as no other game has ever done before. It promotes continuous learning. Teaching and learning from others is as much a part of the game as building a shelter or fighting creepers. While playing in creative mode, with an unlimited supply of every block in their inventory available, players have the freedom to explore their imagination. Players monitor their inventories, conduct ongoing needs assessments, and consider options to expand and improve their character's status in the game. By learning more skills and discovering or crafting more resources, players better prepare themselves for each day, and the reward for their hard work is enhanced playability. When playing in survival mode, players must rely upon a varied and changing set of skills to achieve their immediate and long-term goals.

Minecraft encourages numerous positive traits and builds life skills and spatial understanding. Players develop problem-solving strategies for surviving each night while setting and prioritizing goals for the next day. Food is important, but so is shelter. Armor and weapons will help fight off mobs but require specific and often hard-to-find resources and crafting. It is only through perseverance and planning that players will be successful.

Further, players value the craftsmanship and skills of others while sharing knowledge and innovations, especially in creative multiplayer mode. They develop large-scale, imaginative, team-oriented projects and break down tasks to assign pieces to players based on skill sets. This interdependence builds positive relationships and flexible thinkers.

The vast amount of creative and humorous storytelling and adventure sharing online reflects Minecraft's popularity. Thousands of websites and YouTube videos are dedicated to design tutorials, building, and gameplay strategies. Survival tips, creative ideas, and answers to player questions are only a click or two away on the Internet. Younger players follow and often imitate their favorite YouTube stars, producing and sharing videos and tutorials of their own and emulating a business model for the twenty-first century.

MINECRAFT IN SCHOOLS

Educators are using Minecraft as a tool for learning in most grade levels and content areas in classrooms around the world, and have discovered that their students remain engaged, highly motivated, and excited to share their expertise while demonstrating their learning as they use a favorite game.

The game's encouragement of sharing ideas and seeking help via a thriving and popular Google Group energizes educators as well. Some teachers create and share Minecraft worlds and the associated lesson plans that target specific concepts, skills, and units of study. Some worlds come complete with buildings and nonplayer characters ready for students to explore and interact with. Other teachers design worlds for focused student or team collaboration and task students with building out the world to meet content objectives. Educators are also connecting classrooms globally through large-scale team builds and exploration, with multiple schools learning in a single world designed by a team of teachers.

The scale of every block in Minecraft represents 1 cubic meter, so applications in mathematics and geometry are clear. Students can visualize concepts such as area, perimeter, and volume in three dimensions. Students can demonstrate ratio, proportion, and fractions using Minecraft, as well as collect and graph data, all in the game world. Science teachers have discovered they can use Minecraft to teach geology, physics, and biology. Students are aptly creating models of plate tectonics, DNA, animal cells, and even quantum behavior. Redstone blocks in Minecraft release a power source that students and teachers can use to explore electrical circuitry and operate switches, pistons, and logic gates. One popular modification teaches computer programming, while another supports environmental education.

Minecraft is also great for teaching social sciences and literacy. Students demonstrate their understanding of setting, plot, theme, and conflict by recreating children's stories and young adult novels scene by scene. Books and journals within the game can support student- and teacher-generated text and can include live links to information available on the Internet.

Historical figures can come alive in Minecraft and interact with students in ways traditional textbooks cannot. By role-playing with characters from history, students can experience the wonders of ancient Greece or explore a Civil War battlefield with a virtual soldier and then reflect on their adventures through journal writing and interactions with each other.

With Minecraft, students and educators are free to recreate settings of stories and events regardless of time and space.

Command blocks automate in-game processes like teleportation, item sharing, and gameplay conditions, which leaves the teacher more time for working with students.

GAMIFICATION

Gamification is the process of applying game design principles to out-of-game activities. Game design principles include things like leveling up, gaining points, earning badges, and planning strategy; they do not have to include a competitive component. These principles get players more engaged and motivated, and they have numerous applications in the home setting. Throughout the book you will find examples of how to gamify your family activities, based on the tasks for the in-game portion. For example, in the last lab, Mushroom Stew, players are encouraged to draw the recipe ingredients in a blank crafting table. Drawing the ingredients is in a way gamifying the cooking process and creating the connection between in-game cooking and out-of-game cooking.

As a way of gamifying the quests and labs, you'll find stickers in the back of this book that double as badges. The badges are simple signs that let you and others know that you've completed the quests and labs. Imagine that each lab is a level and for every level completed you earn a sticker badge. Place the badge on the lab once you've completed the family activity and the Minecraft build. You also have access to the digital version of the stickers, which you can include in your family blog. Turn to the section on sharing to learn more about family blogging. Gamifying is all about having fun. So have fun gamifying the quests and labs while crafting with your favorite Minecraft players.

Once you've completed both the family activity (left), and the Minecraft build (center),
place the corresponding sticker (found at the back of the book) on the Lab page.

HOW TO USE THIS BOOK

Each of the four labs within the six quests has both an in-game and an out-of-game activity, which is called the "family activity." Most labs suggest doing the out-of-game activities first as a way to research and prepare for in-game building. Flip through the quests to get a feel for the flow of the book.

You can either work through the labs sequentially, or you can bounce from one lab to another. If you're new to Minecraft, consider starting at the beginning, as Quest 1 introduces basic gameplay. You can also use the labs to connect your child's love of the game with an out-of-game learning experience. For example, if you're planning to visit a museum, consider skipping to Quest 4, The Arts, whose labs are a perfect fit for that experience. Quest 6, however, is best left until you've completed most, if not all, of the other labs, as it's a culmination of your work in the book.

Use this book as a bridge between Minecraft players (usually kids) and their nonplayer counterparts (typically parents or teachers). Sit down with your children and pick a place to start. We want this book to open and build communication, collaboration, creativity, and critical thinking between kids and adults. Nonplayers will learn about Minecraft, while players will enjoy learning about analog, community, and other out-of-game connections.

We encourage you to start building in Minecraft with your kids to further develop your bond. Minecraft is an immersive experience that naturally offers opportunities to try, fail, and try again. Use those same principles as you work with your Minecraft player on the out-of-game part of each lab.

MINECRAFT BASICS

What Is Minecraft?

Minecraft is a game. Yet, since its inception in 2009, it has evolved into an amazing tool for creating, innovating, teaching, and learning. It absorbs players in a blocky, three-dimensional world where they are free to explore and create whatever they can think of using a simple interface. With over seventy million copies sold, it is quickly becoming the world's all-time best-selling game.

Minecraft is a unique game in that there are no levels that you pass to continue on inside the game. The game is open-ended, where you create the experience for yourself as you play. The basics of playing Minecraft encourage collaboration and not competition. Certainly players can turn the game into a competitive experience, by playing player versus player (PvP) or racing through a parkour map. When playing in "survival" mode, players gain experience (XP) in a variety of skills.

Single Player vs. Multiplayer

You can play Minecraft alone or with others; and there's no difference in the in-game mechanics between the two. Purchasing a Minecraft account allows players to play in either mode, but it also depends on the platform (see page 14). All players must have their own license and, generally, their own copy of the game for the platform they are using. Some exceptions include console editions.

Playing in single player mode is a solitary yet interactive experience commonly used by players to hone their skills or develop worlds or maps without the potential for interruption from others. Individuals can open or otherwise share their worlds at any time with other players.

In multiplayer mode, players interact with each other, often-times collaborating to achieve common goals and develop strategies for expansion and resource accumulation. Through cooperative play and experimentation, players polish their skills in areas like redstone mining, building, and food production. Compared to most other games, Minecraft removes the arguing often associated with playing collaboratively.

Creative Mode and Survival Mode

Players must decide between two common game mode options when beginning a new game: creative mode and survival mode. (You may hear players talk about a third option for play known as adventure mode. This mode preserves structures and special modifications and limits destructive behaviors or "griefing" [see "Learn to Speak Minecraft," page 17] from visitors to the map.)

In "creative" mode, every player has access to an unlimited supply of blocks of every kind. They can fly high in the air and dive deep under water without fear of dying. Players cannot harm others or be killed or attacked by mobs; they don't need to eat or worry about their health. They can concentrate instead on creating whatever their minds can think of. When playing in this mode with others, builds can reach epic proportions.

When first playing in "survival" mode, players quickly discover that they need to feed themselves and avoid falls from high places to stay healthy. Loss of health due to hunger or physical activity will eventually lead to death. They will also discover that when nighttime comes, they are susceptible to attack by monsters like zombies and creepers.

Players in survival mode begin play with nothing and, through exploration of their environment, gather resources like wood and stone. They then craft these blocks into tools, weapons, and other useful items. They must construct a shelter to keep the monsters out at night and acquire food by killing animals or harvesting seeds and growing crops. As days and nights pass, players become more proficient at gathering resources and crafting items. Weapons and armor protect players from monsters, allowing them to travel at night and explore more of their unique world.

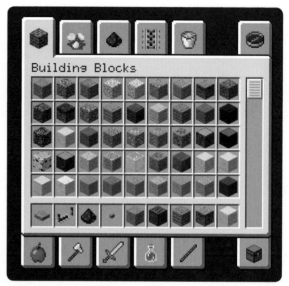

Players in creative mode have unlimited access to all blocks.

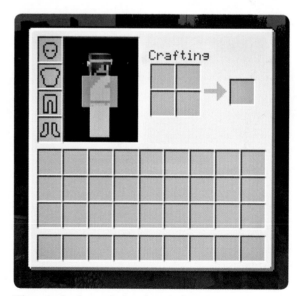

When playing in survival mode, your inventory starts completely empty. Begin by punching trees to collect wood. Each box is ready to store the materials you mine.

VERSIONS AND PLATFORMS

Minecraft was originally developed as a game for the PC, but it's now available in several versions and can be played on multiple platforms. See the list below to discover the similarities and differences among the various platforms and versions.

It's important to note that worlds and maps created using one platform may not be playable in a different platform, and that in order to play with others in multiplayer mode, all players need to be using the same platform *and* version.

	PC PLATFORM	CONSOLE	POCKET EDITION PE
OPERATING SYSTEM OR DEVICE	Windows, Mac, Linux	Xbox, PlayStation, WiiU	Android, iOS, Windows 10 Windows Phone
FEATURES	The original, full version of Minecraft containing all blocks, special features, and craftable items	A mostly full-featured, earlier version of the original	An abridged version of the original designed for the limitations of small touchscreens
MULTIPLAYER?	Yes, full integration	Yes, available via the Xbox or PlayStation network	Yes, via local network or online PE server
KEY LIMITATIONS	None	Limits to world size, number of players, and player skins	Crafting options; no hunger or other dimensions

Playing in multiplayer mode means that all the players in your group will need to join one Minecraft server. There are two options available for this:

- Connect with each other through a Local Area Network (LAN). One player starts the world, selects the option to open it to a LAN, and receives an address to share with other players. The other players launch Minecraft and type in this address to join the game.

- Connect through one of numerous online servers, which usually require a monthly fee to join. Minecraft.net offers a hosted option known as Minecraft Realms at a modest price and is a good choice for family play. You connect to an online server in similar fashion to a LAN—sign up for the service and connect to it through the Minecraft launcher.

How to Play

This section references the default keystrokes and mouse options for playing Minecraft on a PC. This is the version most adults favor. You can find instructions and commands for other platforms by searching Minecraft.gamepedia.com.

Minecraft does not come with any directions or instructions. After launching the game for the first time and selecting creative or survival mode, you appear at a random location in a randomly generated world. That's it. You must figure out the rest—which is what most kids do. They voraciously consume information about the game and its features by watching hours of YouTube videos, reading page after page of tips and strategies on the web, and comparing notes with their friends while playing.

It's our hope that you engage your children's passion for learning everything they can about Minecraft and ask them to become your teacher or mentor. We designed our labs to showcase their expertise yet keep you in a comfortable place as a learner.

Lesson 1: Small Steps

You don't need to know everything about this game before you play it. Enjoy the time you spend playing Minecraft with the young ones in your life and be open to their guidance. We suggest playing for the first time in survival mode. Ask your young teacher to set the world to peaceful so that monsters are not active. This will give you more time to practice.

1. After launching the game, press W to move forward.
2. Press A to slide to the left.
3. Press D to slide to the right
4. Press S to take a step backward.
5. Tap the spacebar to hop in the air. If there is a block in front of you, press W *and* spacebar to jump on top of it.
6. If you are playing in creative mode, double tap the spacebar and you will fly in the air. Hold down the spacebar and press W at the same time to fly up and forward.
7. Press and hold the shift button to land.

There are numerous options for customizing each player's controls. Beginners should stick with the basic movement keys of W, A, S, and D.

Lesson 2: Movement

The mouse is used to control where your head is looking. Move the mouse left to look left. Move it right to look right. Now let's try some combinations.

1. Press and hold W *while* moving the mouse to the left. You'll travel forward several steps to the left.
2. Repeat, but move to the right now. You'll travel forward several steps to the right.

Lesson 3: Breaking and Placing Blocks

By now, you'll have discovered that objects are likely blocking your path. You'll use the two buttons on your mouse to first break and then place blocks. You can break and place blocks up to five blocks away. You can't break or place any blocks directly beneath you without hopping first.

1. Find a tree or block of sand or soil, walk up to it, and look directly at the block. Aim the tiny crosshairs (+) at the block and hold down the left click button on your mouse until the block breaks.
2. Move forward and the block will pop into one of your inventory slots (on the tool belt) at the bottom of the screen. Break several more blocks until you get the hang of it.
3. Now let's place a block. Put a block in your right hand by selecting the number of the slot in your inventory that corresponds to the block. You have nine slots in your tool belt.
4. Locate a spot where you would like to place that block, line up the crosshairs, and right-click.

▪ Lesson 4: Inventory

You've now learned how to move, jump on top of blocks, and break and place blocks. To return to the settings screen, press the ESC key. This is where you quit the game. Press ESC again to go back to the game.

1. Now press E to see your inventory. If you are playing in survival mode, you'll discover the blocks you have mined are located in your tool belt, but you'll also see more available slots above the original nine. This is your backpack area. Drag and drop a few blocks from your tool belt to the backpack. Blocks stored in your backpack are always available by pressing E.
2. If you are playing in creative mode, you'll discover that you have access to *all* the Minecraft blocks. Scroll through your inventory and click on the tabs to see all of the blocks and items. Drag blocks you wish to place into your tool belt for easy access.

Congratulations! You now have enough information to explore your new world. Head off, and with a little help and guidance, build a shelter, craft some useful items, find some food, and enjoy the sunset. Once you've gotten the basics, you can customize your controls. When you are ready to learn more, visit Minecraftopia. com for information, tips, and crafting recipes presented in a clean, visual style.

ONLINE RESOURCE

To see an example of what a team of builders can accomplish in creative mode, watch any of these videos from FyreUK: *https://goo.gl/C1BYQc.*

Learn to Speak Minecraft

It may appear that Minecraft players are speaking a language of their own. Here are a few key terms explained.

Bedrock: Everyone loves digging in Minecraft, but eventually you'll hit bottom. Bedrock is the bottom layer—you cannot break bedrock in survival mode.

Biome: Every Minecraft world has multiple biomes, or ecological regions. Fly around enough in creative mode and you will come across deserts, mountain ranges, oceans, jungles, plains, and many others.

Crafting table: Players use a crafting table to "craft" or create artifacts used in the game.

Creeper: An especially sneaky monster that loves to waddle up next to you and explode.

The End: You can play Minecraft in a sort of sequential order. You begin with nothing in survival mode, become powerful through experience and by crafting resources and then, if you still need a challenge, a final battle against a dragon awaits in another dimension known as The End.

Enderman: A tall, dark, skinny monster that will leave you alone—unless you look into its purple eyes.

Griefer/Griefing: Some players like to join a multiplayer server and sneak around, destroy stuff, and take your things. These are griefers. Nobody likes griefers.

Mobs: These are all the creatures you'll discover while playing Minecraft. There are friendly mobs such as chickens and sheep, neutral mobs like Enderman, and hostile mobs like creepers, zombies, and skeletons.

Mods: The creative team behind Minecraft have opened up the game to other developers by allowing them to create modifications to the original game. These modifications are mostly free and change the game by adding new features or modifying existing ones.

Nether: You can access this scary underworld by building a special portal.

PvP (Player vs. Player): When playing with this feature enabled, players may harm and even kill each other. There is a widely popular Minecraft mini-game based on the popular book series *The Hunger Games*.

Redstone: A special block in Minecraft that releases dust when broken and can be used to provide power to crafted items like pistons and automated doors.

Skin: The fashionable outfit that your character is wearing. Skins are highly customizable in the PC version of Minecraft. Visit minecraftskins.com for hundreds of examples.

Spawn: This is the location where everyone will initially arrive in a new world. Your spawn point changes once you create a home with a bed and lay in it. When you die in survival mode, you will respawn at this point.

Steve: The generic character everyone begins life as. Mojang, the company that created the game, has recently allowed players to choose between Steve and Alex, a female character.

World: When you create a new game, Minecraft generates a unique world for you to play in. You can save, delete, or share worlds with others.

SHARING LABS AND QUESTS

Sharing builds is integral to the Minecraft experience. Some players share by inviting others to play in their world; others take screenshots and make videos. This section of the book offers some suggestions on how and where to share Minecraft creations.

YouTube

Want to help your Minecraft-loving counterpart be the next Stampy or PrestonPlayz? We've got some quick tips on how to get going. If you have a Google account, you already have a YouTube account. If your Minecraft player is under thirteen, we suggest creating a joint Google account. Use the joint account to upload and share videos. Adam Clarke often plays with his son, Django, while making Minecraft videos; check out his channel at youtube.com/user/adamgorgeous.

It's easy to upload your content to share with the Minecraft community. Here are some ways to make a successful video for YouTube:

Edit the video. YouTube has a decent video editor built into the platform. Go to YouTube.com/editor. From the editor you can clip sections, add music and text, and even annotate the videos. Annotations are clickable pop-up boxes that allow viewers to subscribe or be redirected to an outside website.

Choose the music. Most music is copyrighted and not free to reuse or add to your video. In the YouTube video editor, you can access free music to add to your videos. Another great place to find free music is the Creative Commons Music site at http://creativecommons.org/legalmusicforvideos. Of course, you can always create your own music.

Would you watch it? One of the best benchmarks for good videos is to ask yourself, "Would I watch it?" This simple question is quite powerful. You watched the video as you edited it, but would you watch the video if you didn't know who had created it? If you're not sure, upload your video and make it unlisted. Share your unlisted video with other family and friends to get feedback.

The audience is tough. If you feel like you need to make excuses for your video, redo the video. The audience on YouTube is typically pretty tough on videos that should have been edited better. Watch other videos with a critical eye to learn more.

Video settings. Choose your visibility setting when uploading your videos. YouTube gives three choices: public, unlisted, and private. Public videos are easily searchable by anyone online, unlisted videos are not searchable but can be easily shared with the video link, and private videos can only be viewed by you.

Allow or disallow comments. If you are making videos public and are concerned about negative comments, consider leaving comments off. Under your channel, select the video you've uploaded. You can control whether viewers can leave comments. Go to advanced settings to find the option to turn off comments. It's also possible to review comments before they are posted.

Tag your video. Be sure to tag your Minecraft videos with #minecrafterbook. See page 21 for more information.

Screencasting

Screencasting is how your favorite YouTubers record their game-play. The screencasting tool is different for every device you play on. There are several free or inexpensive options for screencasting for PC and tablets. It's a little different if you want to record from a console. Here's a list:

- **Windows/Mac**

    Camtasia $

    Adobe Captivate $$$

    Screencast-O-Matic free

- **Tablet**

Between the time of writing and publishing, there will likely be even more apps available. We suggest doing a search for "screencasting" or "record screen." When you find one you like, please share it with the rest of the #minecrafterbook community.

- **Console**

To record on a console you need to buy an extra piece of hardware. The devices go by a couple of different names: GameDVR and Game Capture. Both terms will get you the same device. The device is installed between the console and screen.

Screenshots

Screenshots are pictures of the device screen. Every device has a way of snapping a picture of what is on the screen. We've listed some examples of how to grab a screenshot below; please note that your device may be different.

- **PC**

Press F2 to grab a screenshot inside the game. Once the screenshot is taken you'll see text in the chat area that lets you know the filename. To find the screenshots on a Windows machine, go to %appdata%\.minecraft\screenshots. On a Mac, go to Library/ Application Support/ minecraft/screenshots.

- **Tablet**

For Apple products, press and hold both the home button and the power button simultaneously. The image is saved in your camera roll. Android varies based on the operating system. Typically, hold the down volume key and the power button at the same time. The screenshot will be saved in the gallery.

- **Console**

For Xbox, double tap the Xbox button, then the Y button. For PlayStation, press and hold the share button for at least one second.

Blogging

Start a blog to hold screenshots of your creations as you work through this book. Blogging is a great way to include more learning and exploration as you play and make your creations visible and helpful to others.

The best blogs encourage others to create and think. John keeps a blog of the builds he does with his students at http://edtecworks.com. Both Google Blogger and Weebly.com offer a free and easy-to-use blogging platform.

#minecrafterbook

Use the hashtag #minecrafterbook as you share and publish your work online. We love to see what you create in and out of Minecraft. Tweet @minecrafterbook and we'll retweet your work. Using hashtags and Twitter handles will help build a community of people working through the quests and labs.

Using Your Inventory

In this quest, you'll be using all the blocks in your inventory. Start with the basics and strengthen your skills.

There's no right way to play Minecraft. It's a sandbox game—meaning that it's open-ended rather than structured—where players are free to explore, mine, and craft their experiences.

The act of mining is one of the key activities in Minecraft, and looking for the right blocks, or materials, can sometimes feel like a digital scavenger hunt. In the family activity, you'll hunt for real-life versions of items you'll find inside the game.

Crafting is the second key activity of the game. For the Minecraft part of this lab, you'll use resources you mine to craft useful items to make living and crafting more fun. You'll start at the beginning by punching trees and move toward crafting tools and a shelter, which is how everyone starts playing.

Family Activity: Scavenger Hunt

A scavenger hunt is a fun way to get your hands dirty while looking for the items on the list. Be sure to work together, as some of the items might be difficult to spot.

■ **APPROXIMATE TIME TO COMPLETE**
45 minutes

■ **MATERIALS**
Scavenger Hunt Checklist
   (see page 133 for the complete list)
Timer

1. **Share the scavenger hunt list on page 31 with your team. Consider how you can work together to tackle the list quickly. This is a time challenge, too!**

2. **Set the timer for 45 minutes and begin.**

3. **Once the time is up, add up the number of items you found.**

MORE TO EXPLORE
Another way to play: You and your team can keep the list handy during the week and take pictures of the items whenever and wherever you find them. Post the craziest pictures (especially the spider eye) to your blog or social media with the hashtag #minecrafterbook.

SCAVENGER HUNT CHECKLIST

☐ Apple
☐ Bed
☐ Boat
☐ Bow and arrow
☐ Bread
☐ Cactus
☐ Cake
☐ Carpet
☐ Carrot
☐ Coal or charcoal
☐ Cobweb
☐ Compass

☐ Flower pot
☐ Flowers
☐ Furnace
☐ Gold
☐ Glass
☐ Grass
☐ Gravel
☐ Hoe
☐ Ice or snow
☐ Iron
☐ Ladder
☐ Leather

☐ Pumpkin pie
☐ Saddle
☐ Sand
☐ Shovel
☐ Sign
☐ Spider eye
☐ Sponge
☐ Stairs
☐ Sticks
☐ Stone
☐ String
☐ Sugar
☐ Tree

Every block, or material, that's mined in the game has a hardness level that determines which tool is best for breaking it. You can break most blocks by hand, without any tools, but using the right tool will save you lots of time. The general rules of thumb for using tools are shown at right.

Every player starts out with nothing in his or her inventory. The objective is to collect resources to craft a full set of tools so you can mine harder blocks to craft even stronger tools. Once you've collected some blocks, craft new tools and resources to make play even better. Grab a tool and start breaking blocks!

■ **GAME MODE**
Survival

■ **APPROXIMATE TIME TO COMPLETE**
1+ hours in Minecraft

■ **PLATFORMS**
PC/Mac, Consoles, Pocket Edition (PE)

1. **When you first enter the game, you'll start at spawn point. Look around to see what types of resources are nearby. Start mining by punching trees to gather wood.**

2. **Turn the wood you've gathered into a crafting table, which allows you to craft all the tools available in the game (fig. 1). Without a crafting table, you're limited to crafting very few items. It's helpful to have multiple crafting tables. Put one in your house, one in your mineshaft (where the player mines underground for more resources), and one where you're harvesting trees. Start using your crafting table by turning your wood into tools (fig. 2).**

3. **Build a shelter. Your shelter could be on top of a hill made from dirt or inside a mountain surrounded by stone blocks. If you're playing in survival mode, the goal is to build a shelter to protect you from monsters.**

TOOLS CHEAT SHEET

 Axes: for mining and crafting anything made from wood

 Pickaxes: for mining and crafting stone or harder materials

 Shovels: for mining and crafting dirt

 Hoes: for preparing the ground for planting

 Weapons (such as swords): for killing mobs and animals

HARDNESS →

HANDS (NO TOOLS)	WOOD	STONE	IRON	GOLD	DIAMOND

The harder the material a tool is made from, the faster it will break blocks.

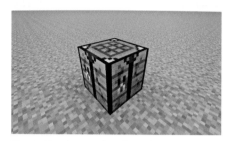

Fig. 1: Use the wood you've mined to create a crafting table.

Fig. 2: Use your crafting table and some wood to craft new tools, like the wooden pickaxe shown.

Fig. 3: Build a bed using three blocks of wool and three wood planks.

Fig. 4: Place the bed in a safe place, such as inside your shelter.

Fig. 5: The crafting recipe for a chest.

Fig. 6: Chests are a great place to store extra resources.

4. Craft a bed, if possible. You'll need three blocks of wool ("mined" from sheep) of any color and three wood planks (fig. 3). Place the bed in a safe place, preferably inside a home (fig. 4). You can break the bed and take it with you when exploring further from home. If you don't make a bed, you can either hide out in your shelter or keep mining and fight any monsters that come your way.

5. Crafting a chest (fig. 5) is a great way to keep extra items (fig. 6). Ask your co-player whether crafting a chest is necessary. (In survival mode, players must craft all their resources; if they die, players lose all items in their inventory—unless they have placed them in the chest. In creative mode, players don't need chests, as you can't die and always have access to unlimited items.) Placing two chests next to each other creates one large chest.

MORE TO EXPLORE

Minecraft was originally called Cave Game. Markus Persson, also known as Notch, started the game with the simple premise of mining to craft. The version you'll play today has more tools, blocks, and resources than any previous version.

It's Electric!

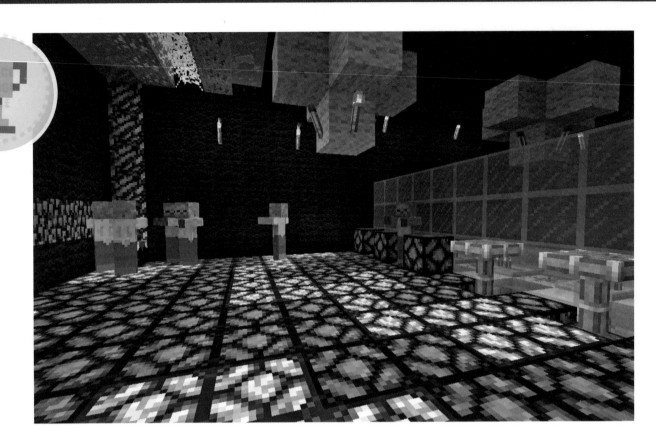

This lab is all about creating and conducting electricity. For the family activity, try your hand at creating a simple electrical circuit. For the Minecraft play, we explore redstone, which is used to create and conduct power. We use redstone dust to make a light-up dance floor and a disco ball, and to automate moving attractions. The goal is to create a party worthy of a mob—in this case, a mob of zombies. Zombies aren't always hostile—be sure to play in creative mode so they can't harm you!

ONLINE RESOURCE

Check out this website to play with designing more complex circuits:
http://www.123dapp.com/circuits

Family Activity: Simple Circuit

■ **APPROXIMATE TIME TO COMPLETE**

1 hour

■ **MATERIALS**

Wire cutter

3-volt LED bulb

Button, coin, or watch cell battery

Electrical tape

Miniature toggle switch

Double-ended alligator clips
(two clips connected by a wire)

Explore the basics of electricity with this fun project, in which you'll build a simple circuit using an LED light. You can purchase all the items you need at a hardware store.

1. **Gather your materials (fig. 1). Use the wire cutter to expose the ends of both wires on the LED bulb. Trim the wires just enough so they're easy to work with, but without leaving too much wire exposed (fig. 2).**

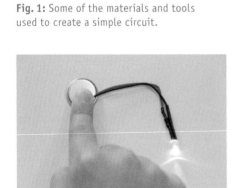

Fig. 1: Some of the materials and tools used to create a simple circuit.

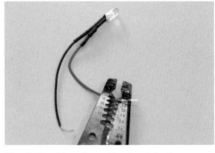

Fig. 2: Use the wire cutter to strip the very ends of the LED bulb's wires.

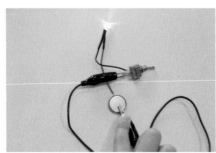

Fig. 3: Light the bulb by connecting the positive and negative wires to the corresponding sides of the battery.

Fig. 4: Add a switch to turn the light on and off.

MORE TO EXPLORE
- How can you change or adapt your simple LED circuit into something different?
- What happens when you use other types of batteries, like AA or AAA?
- What happens when you add another switch to the circuit?

2. **To make the bulb light up, connect the red (positive) wire to the positive side of the battery (the top cap), and the black (negative) wire to the negative side of the battery (the bottom cap). Use some electrical tape to make it stick (fig. 3).**

3. **To turn the bulb on and off, connect the bulb's black wire to one pole of the switch. Connect one of the black alligator clips to the other switch pole, and the other to the negative side of the battery (fig. 4).**

In this part of the lab, we create the decorations for a zombie party using redstone to build two different types of redstone clocks. These "clocks" are actually repeating circuits powered by redstone. One clock is used to power redstone lamps and sticky pistons (which can both push and pull blocks) to create a light-up dance floor, and the other is used to make a light-up entryway to the party.

■ **GAME MODE**
Creative

■ **APPROXIMATE TIME TO COMPLETE**
2–3 hours in Minecraft; 15–30 minutes outside of Minecraft

■ **PLATFORMS**
PC/Mac, Consoles

SHARE YOUR WORK
Use the hashtag *#minecrafterbook* to share your work—we want to see what you've created! Share both your simple LED circuit and your Minecraft dance party.

1. **Choose a flat world, then pick an area that will work for your dance club. To make the dance floor, dig out the floor at least two blocks down. Make a redstone clock using minecart rail, detector rail, powered rail, redstone torch, minecart, and redstone dust. Every revolution the cart makes sends a signal through the detector rail. The detector rail uses redstone dust to carry the signal to redstone lamps (on the left) and sticky pistons (on the right) (fig. 1).**

2. **Place pressure plates all around the floor. Pressure plates have redstone functionality built into them. Once you have most of the floor covered, spawn several silverfish on top of the pressure plates and below the redstone lamps. The slippery bugs will light up the dance floor by activating the pressure plates as they roam around their dance floor cage (fig. 2). Place the redstone lamp above the plates, leaving enough room for the silverfish.**

ABOUT REDSTONE
Redstone is a main power source in Minecraft. It is like electricity and can transmit energy up to fifteen blocks away, though the energy weakens as it's transmitted over a distance.

3. **To make a disco ball, we added flickering redstone torches to prismarine brick blocks (fig. 3).**

4. **Finish your party by adding walls, other decorations, and music. We added a lighted entryway using redstone dust, redstone repeaters, and redstone torch to create another type of redstone clock. Put redstone dust in your hand, break the torch, and quickly replace the torch with redstone dust. (fig. 4). The zombies we invited can't wait for the party to start (fig. 5).**

Fig. 1: Redstone dust "wires" running from the minecart clock activate the redstone lamps and sticky pistons.

Fig. 2: Place pressure plates on the ground, then spawn silverfish to activate them.

Fig. 3: The flashing redstone torches on the disco ball.

Fig. 4: We used another type of redstone clock to light up the entryway.

Fig. 5: Zombie guests queuing up to enter the dance party.

MORE TO EXPLORE

There are literally dozens of other ways to create a party in Minecraft. Have fun improvising!

- We were inspired to create a zombie party, but you can invite any Minecraft character you like. Villagers look pretty funny with their arms crossed on the dance floor.
- What other party features could you include? How about a smoke machine? How can you add pyrotechnics to your party?
- How would your party be different in survival mode?
- What other mobs could you use to activate the pressure plates?

ONLINE RESOURCES

- Check out Jesper the End's Minecraft disco party: *https://youtu.be/MLAoVwR4d80*
- Here's a YouTube playlist to help inspire you: *https://goo.gl/nHMWpY*

Setting a Trap

Kids love devising traps to snare the bad guys in Minecraft. Simple and efficient traps can be made quickly with just a few resources, while more advanced versions can take hours to design and build. To prepare for this challenge, the family activity will show players how to create a colorful Chinese finger trap.

 ONLINE RESOURCE

For a tutorial on how to braid a finger trap, watch this YouTube video: *https://goo.gl/qn9eV7*

Family Activity: Chinese Finger Trap

The Chinese finger trap is a classic novelty toy that can confound those who try to escape its clutches. In this activity, each family member will make his or her own finger trap.

■ **APPROXIMATE TIME TO COMPLETE**

1 hour

■ **MATERIALS**

Scissors
Construction paper in at least 2 colors
Transparent tape or glue
A thick marker or stick to braid the paper around

1. Cut four strips of paper, each approximately 12 inches (30.5 cm) long and 1 inch (2.5 cm) wide (fig. 1).

2. Tape or glue the ends of each pair of strips together at an angle of slightly less than 90 degrees (fig. 2).

3. To hold them temporarily in place, tape the corner of one pair of strips to the end of the marker or stick, then tape the second pair to the opposite side. Contrasting colors should appear next to each other, and the strips should be aligned (fig. 3).

Fig. 1: Cut four strips of paper.

Fig. 2: Tape the ends of each pair of strips together at a nearly 90-degree angle.

Fig. 3: Tape each pair of strips on opposite sides of the marker.

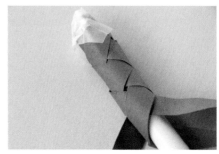

Fig. 4: Alternating colors, braid the strips around the marker.

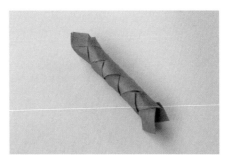

Fig. 5: Trim and finish the braided ends with tape or glue. Remove the marker and secure the top of the trap with tape or glue.

4. Alternating colors, braid the strips around the marker or stick until you reach the end (fig. 4).

5. Use scissors to trim the braided ends, then tape or glue them together. Remove the tape from the end of the marker or stick. Pull the marker out of the center of the finger trap. Finish the ends with tape or glue (fig. 5).

Minecraft Play: Build a Zombie Trap

Lava is a block that's typically found deep underground, in pools of oozing magma, though sometimes it occurs above ground (in the Overworld) in lakes. Lava has many uses, but it's a well-known feature of monster traps. In this part of the lab, you'll build a beginner-level trap—a lava pit of doom—to lure, capture, and destroy hostile mobs and monsters.

■ **GAME MODE**
Build in creative or survival mode; play in survival mode

■ **APPROXIMATE TIME TO COMPLETE**
1–2 hours in Minecraft

■ **PLATFORMS**
PC/Mac, Consoles, PE

1. Use a shovel to dig a pit three blocks by three blocks by three blocks. Place bedrock on the bottom of your pit to ensure that the lava will stay in place (fig. 1).

2. Locate a lava bucket in your inventory. Use the lava bucket to pour lava into the pit. Right-click to place the lava in the center of the bottom of the pit (fig. 2).

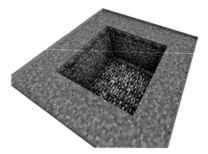

Fig. 1: Dig a pit and place bedrock on the bottom.

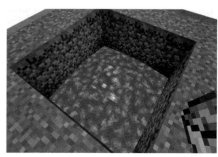

Fig. 2: Pour the lava into the pit.

IT'S A TRAP!
These are some other Minecraft resources that are commonly used by trap makers:

- Arrow dispensers
- Pistons
- Pressure plates
- Sand
- TNT
- Trapdoors
- Tripwire
- Water

ONLINE RESOURCES
The Minecraft Wiki is a great resource for trap ideas and for tutorials on building advanced traps: *http://goo.gl/ZVX7mu*

3. Place dirt or grass blocks over the pit and put a trapdoor in the center. Position the trapdoor hinge opposite from the direction the monster will be approaching. Place a stone pressure plate in front of the trapdoor. In our build, the lava and the wall of the pit appear beneath the trapdoor (fig. 3).

4. Create a solid corridor that runs past the trap with a dead end just beyond it. Now it's time to place the bait— that's you! Get a monster to follow you down the corridor, and as you approach the pressure plate, leap to the other side. The monster will follow you, activate the trapdoor, and fall into the lava pit of doom (fig. 4). This basic trap works for both creepers and zombies.

5. Follow the link opposite, right, to discover more advanced ways to trap monsters and capture their loot at the same time.

Fig. 3: Hide the pit with dirt or grass blocks. Place a trapdoor in the center and a pressure plate in front. A creeper approaches!

Fig. 4: Build a corridor around the trap and entice a monster to follow you.

MORE TO EXPLORE

Blocks of obsidian are created when flowing water comes into contact with lava. With obsidian, you can create a nether portal to use as part of your trap.

SHARE YOUR WORK

Sharing imaginative trap designs is very popular online. There are hundreds of examples on YouTube and on blogs. Record the steps you took to create your trap and share them, along with screenshots, on your family blog. Use the hashtag *#minecrafterbook*.

Fire When Ready!

In this lab you'll alternate between dodging marshmallows and firing TNT into a medieval fortress. In the family activity, you'll have some fun building a Popsicle stick catapult, while in Minecraft, you'll get acquainted with one of the more popular blocks in your inventory—TNT! TNT is a special block that, when ignited with flint and steel, will explode and destroy blocks located near it (the image above shows an explosion in process). For more details, see the sidebar "Getting to Know TNT in Minecraft," page 38.

■ **APPROXIMATE TIME TO COMPLETE**
30 minutes

■ **MATERIALS**
7 large Popsicle sticks,
  6 inches (15 cm) long
10 to 12 rubber bands
Plastic spoon
Marshmallows

Family Activity: Marshmallow Catapult

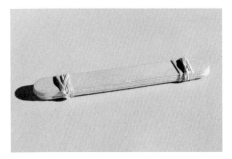

Fig. 1: These stacked sticks will form the base of the catapult.

Fig. 2: Attach the spoon securely to the end of one stick.

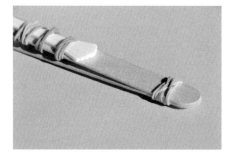

Fig. 3: Attach these two sticks together, making sure to leave one end open.

1. **Stack five sticks on top of each other and secure both ends of the stack with rubber bands (fig. 1).**

2. **Secure the plastic spoon to one of the remaining sticks with at least three rubber bands (fig. 2).**

3. **Attach the remaining stick beneath the stick with the spoon at the bottom only using a rubber band (fig. 3).**

4. **Finally, pry open and then slide the end of the launcher around the stack of sticks and securely attach the two components with rubber bands across the center, as shown in figure 4.**

5. **Load a marshmallow onto your catapult and fire away!**

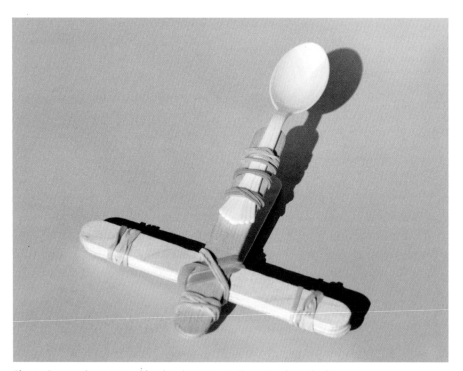

Fig. 4: Cross at least two rubber bands to secure the catapult to the base.

In this part of the lab, you'll build a basic cannon that fires a block of TNT into the distance. The TNT will explode in the air or on the ground. After you've built your first cannon, experiment by adjusting the amount of TNT you use, or build your cannon on the edge of a mountaintop to increase its firing range. See below, right, for more on how TNT works in Minecraft.

Fig. 1: Build two short walls parallel to each other and close off one end.

Fig. 2: Add water to the bottom of the cavity to ensure that the cannon won't explode when the TNT ignites.

■ **GAME MODE**

Creative

■ **APPROXIMATE TIME TO COMPLETE**

2 hours in Minecraft

■ **PLATFORMS**

PC/Mac, Consoles, PE

■ **INVENTORY REQUIREMENTS**

Stone blocks

Bucket of water

Lever or button

Redstone wire

Stone slab

Four redstone repeaters

TNT

 ONLINE RESOURCE

To see what it would be like to be a human cannonball, check out this YouTube video by DanTDM: *https://goo.gl/4Haq7A*

1. Using stone blocks, build two short walls, each one block high and nine blocks long. Build the walls parallel to each other and one block apart. Close off the narrow area between them at one end with another block of stone. The TNT will be launched from the open end (fig. 1).

2. At the closed end of the foundation, place two blocks of stone, one on top of the other. Destroy the block on the bottom (the one touching the ground) and fill the cavity with water. The water should flow all the way to the end of the wall but not beyond it (fig. 2). Adding water to the bottom of the cannon will ensure that it won't explode when the TNT is ignited.

GETTING TO KNOW TNT IN MINECRAFT

Most commonly activated with flint and steel

• Won't destroy blocks under water

• Useful for clearing out large areas

• Use redstone to wire cannons, traps, and other crafty innovations

• Can be placed in a minecart and sent down the rail line as an explosive surprise

• Can be placed next to each other to create colossal explosions

3. Place the lever or button behind the tall block at the closed end of the cannon. Connect the lever to redstone wire. Run the wire along most of the length of both walls. Stop the wire one block short of the end of the wall on the right and two blocks short of the end of the wall on the left (fig. 3).

Fig. 3: Attach a lever to redstone wire. Run the wire along the walls, stopping it one block from the end of the right wall and two blocks from the end of the left wall.

4. At the open end of the cannon, place the slab on top of the water block and add two more stone blocks to the wall to the left of the slab. Add redstone wire on top of those blocks (fig. 4). These blocks will prime the TNT just before it's launched into the air. When primed, or activated with redstone, TNT blocks blink white.

5. Place four repeaters along the left wall and set the delay on each to at least two ticks (fig. 5). Repeaters slow down the signal from the lever just a bit so the TNT block is launched before it explodes.

6. Make sure the redstone lever is disengaged, then fill the water cavity with TNT blocks (fig. 6). Pull the switch! The blocks of TNT will explode, launching the solitary TNT block at the open end of the cannon into the air.

Fig. 4: Place a slab at the open end, add two blocks to the wall on the left, and run redstone wire on top of the blocks.

Fig. 5: Place four repeaters on the left wall. Set the delay on each to at least two ticks.

Fig. 6: Disengage the lever, fill the water cavity with TNT blocks, then pull the switch!

MORE TO EXPLORE

Have each family or team member build a fortress around his or her cannon and see whose can survive the longest. Obsidian is very resistant to explosions. Build and then try to knock down an obsidian tower by firing TNT from multiple cannons.

QUEST 2

Textures, Patterns, and Landscapes

In this quest, discover science in cooking while you design a restaurant, learn about American Southwest patterns in art, create gardens to grow useful crops, and get ready for the tastiest lab.

PLEASE
BE SEATED

There are millions of restaurants, big and small, around the world. Restaurants are designed according to the style of food, culture, and community. Patterns and textures exist inside and outside of restaurants. The floor plan for seats, the layout of each dish, even the assembly of food are all patterns.

To complete this lab, the family activity will have you spend time researching local restaurants to explore all their aspects. In the game, you'll craft a restaurant of your own and design it according to your own taste.

ONLINE RESOURCE

Check out Arch Daily's International Restaurant Design winners:
http://goo.gl/d4v2Mq

Researching local restaurants is a fun way to gather crafting inspiration while filling your mental fuel tank for designing your own in Minecraft (see pages 44–45).

■ **APPROXIMATE TIME TO COMPLETE**
1 hour

■ **MATERIALS**
Camera
Notepad and pencil

1. **Choose a restaurant. Consider one that's opened recently or one you've never been to but have wanted to visit.**

2. **While dining in the restaurant, take photographs of the layout. Make notes about patterns and textures. Consider the floor plan, the types of food and how they're served, and even the locations of the bathrooms.**

3. **Visit one or two other restaurants that are larger or smaller than your first one and that serve different cuisines (figs. 1–3). Take photos and make notes. Consider how they're the same as well as how they're different.**

Fig. 1-3: As you research restaurants and their interiors for your in-game design, take note of their patterns and textures.

Designing and building restaurants in the game is an important way to customize your world. It's fun to invite fellow players to visit your restaurant and enjoy a fresh meal of cooked chicken or even a cake.

■ **GAME MODE**

Creative

■ **APPROXIMATE TIME TO COMPLETE**

2–3 hours in Minecraft

■ **PLATFORMS**

PC/Mac, Consoles, PE

1. Sort through the information you gathered in the family activity and choose the elements you would like to include in your restaurant design. Follow the checklist on the opposite page as you design your own. As you work, stay true to your restaurant theme, but also consider doing something surprising.

2. Choose a location for building your restaurant, one that suits its style. Will your restaurant be surrounded by other businesses in a large city? Could your restaurant be on a mountaintop or near a beach? We built a restaurant that blends the indoors with the outdoors (figs. 1 and 2), with a garden next to the seating.

3. The kitchen is the heart of every restaurant. Decide where yours will be in relation to the dining room. The kitchen for this restaurant is in the back, but the food is out front. Think about how many chests you'll need for storage. The furnace cooks food to perfection (fig. 3).

4. Decide where some of your food will come from. We built a yard for cows and chickens so we could get fresh milk and eggs easily (fig. 4).

5. Think about where the patrons will purchase and consume the food prepared in the kitchen. How much space is required between tables? What kind of pattern is the layout of the floor plan? Is it a simple grid with tables and chairs in rows, or more free-flowing?

6. When you choose a name and create a logo, remember that even logos have patterns in them. The pattern of your logo can be based on size, color, shape, and name. Take care in creating your name and logo. Make both memorable! The best restaurants designers consider theirs carefully.

Fig. 1: In this design, the restaurant's exterior (a garden) and interior (low tables and seats) are part of the same open flow.

Fig. 2: The garden's rows follow a pattern: two rows of garden plants separated by dirt, water, dirt with dandelions, and sunflowers.

Fig. 3: Stock your restaurant kitchen with raw chicken, raw fish, wheat, sugar, and vegetables and store in chests. The furnace cooks food to perfection.

Fig. 4: It may seem strange to have animals near the dining area, but easy access to fresh eggs and milk make up for the barnyard feel.

ONLINE RESOURCE

If you want easy access to food, consider crafting an automatic egg farm. All you need is some redstone, hoppers, chickens, and a few other items. Check out this great tutorial on automatic egg farming: *http://goo.gl/08Oo6h*

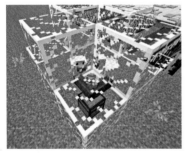

Automatic egg farms allow easy access to fresh eggs without having to chase chickens around the Overworld. Build the walls high enough to keep the chickens from getting out.

MINECRAFT RESTAURANT DESIGN CHECKLIST

☐ **Choose a theme.** A few restaurant themes include fast food, fine dining, family style, and ethnic. Fast food restaurants focus on preparing and serving food quickly, while fine dining restaurants emphasize a custom high-priced menu. Family-style restaurants are casual and typically serve large portions. Ethnic restaurants have menus that originate from a particular culture, such as Mexican, Greek, or Italian. Try mixing up the themes to develop a custom restaurant.

☐ **Decide what kind of food you want to serve.** It can be diet specific, such as vegetarian, vegan, or chicken only. Perhaps the food is from a particular culture?

☐ **Design the space.** The space in a restaurant sets the atmosphere and pace. Some restaurants are dark with individual dining areas; others may be more communally centered with large tables shared with multiple dining parties. When designing the space, be sure to consider the route patrons and servers take when navigating the restaurant.

☐ **Choose an ambience or atmosphere.** High ceilings make the space feel large, airy, and often cold. Smaller spaces can make a restaurant feel cozy, encouraging patrons to sit closely.

☐ **Build the kitchen, dining room, and bathrooms.** Each space requires specific features. Imagine you are using the space as the chef or a patron. Consider how far the chef must travel to complete a dish or how smooth it is for patrons to find their table.

☐ **Build a menu.** Before your patrons get to experience your restaurant they will want to know what food you serve. Pay close attention to the food on your menu.

☐ **Craft a name and logo.** Some restaurants are named after the founder; others might be named after the style of food they serve.

In this lab, we explore creating banners, which you can use as decoration both in and out of Minecraft. In the family activity, play with paper weaving to create a unique design. In Minecraft, explore textures and patterns by designing and creating banners inspired by Native American art from the American Southwest.

Use this paper weaving technique to create a patterned banner. The example shown opposite is a creeper face—the game's blocky, "pixelated" look is a great fit for this technique. Copy our design, get inspired by Native American art opposite, below, or create a design of your own.

■ **APPROXIMATE TIME TO COMPLETE**
30 minutes

■ **MATERIALS**
Scissors
3 sheets of colored paper
   (2 in different colors)
Glue

1. Cut a sheet of paper into 1-inch (2.5-cm) wide strips. The length of the strips will depend on the size of your project. We used two colors to create our weaving (fig. 1), but you can use several; the more colors you use, the more layers you'll weave.

2. Cut a second sheet of paper into strips of the same width, stopping about 1 inch (2.5 cm) from the edge (fig. 2).

3. Weave the loose strips of paper under and over the strips of the second sheet to create your pattern (fig. 3).

4. Check your work as you go, make any final adjustments, then create a frame for your finished weaving by gluing it to a larger sheet of paper (fig. 4).

Fig. 1: Cut a sheet of colored paper into 1-inch (2.5-cm) wide strips.

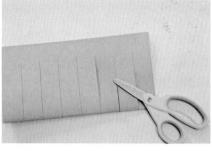

Fig. 2: Cut another sheet into strips, stopping about 1 inch (2.5 cm) from its edge.

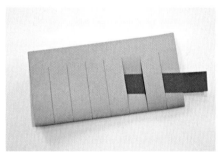

Fig. 3: Create a pattern by weaving the strips over and under each other.

Fig. 4: Glue the finished weaving to a larger sheet.

MORE TO EXPLORE

Native Americans in are generally defined as people whose ancestors lived in North America before the arrival of Columbus. Research the many types of patterns in Native American art and take note of their colors and designs. Recreate a pattern using the paper weaving technique shown above, or use your findings to inspire your own designs.

Use these Native American-inspired patterns as jumping-off points for the activities in this lab.

Banners, or decorative blocks, first appeared in Minecraft 1.8. You can decorate your Minecraft builds with customized banners with unique patterns by mixing colors and patterns.

Patterns occur naturally in Minecraft. Its various *biomes*, or climate-based regions, have different patterns. There are more than sixty unique biomes in Minecraft. In this part of the lab, you'll explore the patterns of the rare Mesa or Bryce biome (see right), a dry biome. The Mesa biome has the most recognizable pattern in the form of colorful layers.

- **GAME MODE**
  Creative

- **APPROXIMATE TIME TO COMPLETE**
  1 hour in Minecraft

- **PLATFORMS**
  PC/Mac, Consoles, PE

- **SEED ACCESS INFORMATION**
  PC/Mac biome seed:
  2347792175013291886
  Xbox/PlayStation seed:
  1522406735809595204
  Pocket Edition seed: *3083210*

A wide shot of the Mesa or Bryce biome, which was released in Minecraft 1.7.2. The colorful blocks are types of clay that are useful in crafting.

1. **Load a seed world with a Mesa biome. (Note that the Mesa biome may not be at spawn, the spot your character starts in-game. Press "e" to access your inventory, where you'll find banners in many color variations (fig. 1).**

2. **You'll need a crafting table to create unique banners (fig. 2).**

Fig. 1: A hot bar full of banners.

Fig. 2: Use a crafting table to customize the banners.

ABOUT MINECRAFT BANNERS
Banners can be placed on the ground and on walls. They aren't solid, so mobs and other items can move through them. They can't be burned, and water and lava flow around them.

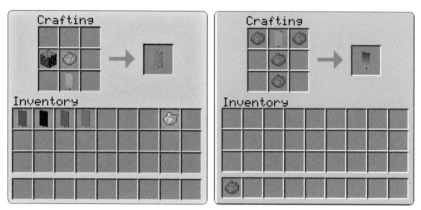

Fig. 3 and 4: Change dye colors to change the color of a pattern.

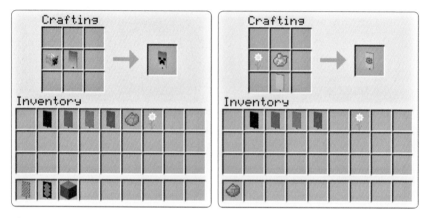

Fig. 5 and 6: You can also customize your banners with images.

3. **Place a banner and other items in the crafting table. For example, you can place a brick block next to a banner to create a brick-like pattern. Add a dye to the recipe to change the pattern's color (figs. 3 and 4). Use dye in a Y-shaped pattern to create a gradient of color on the banner. You can then customize a gradient banner with a creeper head (fig. 5), a daisy (fig. 6), and more.**

MORE TO EXPLORE

- Place the banners you designed on, in, and around your restaurant (see Lab 5). Make the banner a part of the restaurant theme and logo.
- Create large versions of your banners using pixel art. Begin by coloring your pixel art on graph paper, then recreate the drawing in-game using similar colored blocks.
- Create a banner that resembles your country's flag.

PLACE
BADGE
HERE

Crafting cookies in and out of the game make this the
yummiest lab. To complete the family activity, bake
a batch of delicious cookies to explore the science
behind cooking.

   Cookies were the first food in Minecraft that
could be stacked. Stackable food allows you to carry
more when exploring the world. But not all cookies
in Minecraft are edible, as you'll see in the Minecraft
part of this lab.

Cooking is a science. When we combine ingredients like flour, sugar, and butter to make cookies, they change chemically and physically, first as each ingredient is added and mixed, which changes their texture. During baking, cookies go through a chemical change as the butter and other ingredients melt, aligning their atoms in new combinations. That physical change leaves the cookies lumpy with yummy bumps.

- **APPROXIMATE TIME TO COMPLETE**
  45 minutes

- **MATERIALS**
  Your favorite cookie recipes (we made chocolate chip and peanut butter cookies; see the Resources for suggestions on where to find recipes)

1. **Notice the patterns among different cookie recipes. Some require more butter or sugar, while others ask for extras like chocolate chips. The pattern of baking cookies remains the same: prepare dry ingredients, prepare wet ingredients, mix, place dough onto pan, bake, eat, and smile (fig. 1).**

2. **When you make your chocolate chip cookies, notice the changes in texture that happen as the ingredients are mixed and then baked (fig. 2).**

Fig. 1: Notice the changes in texture as you mix the dry and wet ingredients.

3. **Try making peanut butter cookies. Peanut butter cookies generally have patterns on top. Once the peanut butter cookie is on the baking sheet, you can take different utensils like a fork, knife, or spoon to make patterns (fig. 3). Try making a creeper face on your peanut butter cookies.**

4. **Be sure to share your delicious cookies!**

Fig. 2: These baked chocolate chip cookies have a bumpy texture.

Fig. 3: A fork was used to make the texture shown on these peanut butter cookies.

MORE TO EXPLORE
Try making cookies with different textures and shapes.

Crafting cookies in real life is much more delicious than the in-game counterpart, but it can be just as fun. In this part of the lab, create cookies.

- **GAME MODE**

  Survival

- **APPROXIMATE TIME TO COMPLETE**

  1 hour in Minecraft

- **PLATFORMS**

  PC/Mac, Consoles, PE

Fig. 1: Harvest some wheat and cocoa beans and place on a crafting table to make "edible" chocolate chip cookies. (Pocket Edition is shown here.)

1. Craft "edible" Minecraft cookies by harvesting wheat and cocoa beans. You can find cocoa beans hanging on trees in Jungle biomes, which are strewn with vines and trees (fig. 1).

2. Create an oversized chocolate chip cookie (figs. 2 and 3). Study one of your freshly baked cookies. Notice the lumpy top, the different colors, and the uneven shape. Gather blocks, mixing oak wood planks (to get the light brown color) mixed with spruce wood or dark oak wood planks (for chocolate chips).

3. Craft an oversized peanut butter cookie. Use birch wood planks to make the classic peanut butter color. Once you've crafted the shape of the cookie, use more of the blocks to create your own pattern on top. Just like a fresh peanut butter cookie takes a fork to create the grid shape, you can craft any pattern using more blocks (fig. 4).

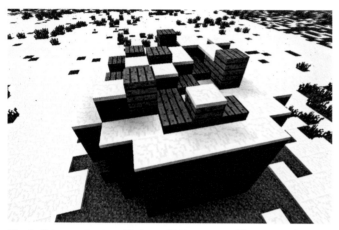

Fig. 2: This oversized cookie has a hidden center. The snow makes it look like powdered sugar was dusted on top.

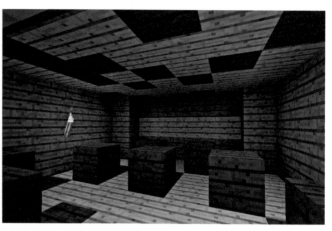

Fig. 3: This oversized cookie has a gooey center. Massive chocolate chips and torches keep the insides extra delicious.

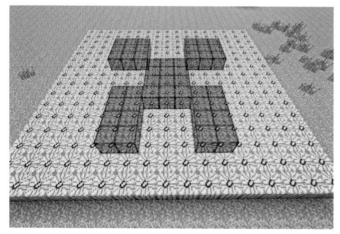

Fig. 4: An oversized "peanut butter" cookie made from pumpkins and glass to resemble a creeper head.

MORE TO EXPLORE

Try making one of your cookies look like a giant iron golem took a bite out of it. Craft other delicious treats, such as a cake or even a pumpkin pie.

 ONLINE RESOURCE

To find a Jungle biome, do a web search for "jungle biome seed."

Plants in Minecraft act similarly to plants out of the game. Both require sufficient sunlight, water, and prepared soil. Both start from seeds and, when harvested, give seeds in return. Plants outside the game use photosynthesis to produce their own food from sunlight. Plants in the game also require sunlight to grow. The farther your plants are from water, the slower they grow. As an example, wheat takes about 40 minutes of gameplay to grow from seed to harvestable crop. Of course, there are ways to make your crops grow faster, in and out of the game.

In this lab, you'll grow plants in and out of the game as a way to connect gameplay with real life.

Family Activity: Planting Seeds

Help your Minecraft-loving counterpart learn about growing plants in this family activity. Pick out seeds appropriate for the growing season, plant them, and observe them as they grow. Try experimenting with different seeds, soil, and water content. Take some time to garden. Whether you're planning a new garden or maintaining an existing one, this lab offers the chance to spend time outdoors.

▨ **APPROXIMATE TIME TO COMPLETE**
   30 minutes

▨ **MATERIALS**
   Pot
   Soil
   Packet of seeds
   Water

1. **Prepare the soil. Fill a garden pot with soil most of the way to the top. The soil should be rich in color and ready for your seeds and water.**

2. **Use a finger or a tool to poke a hole into the soil. Drop a couple of seeds into the hole and cover with soil. Water the seeds and place in sufficient sunlight (fig. 1).**

Fig. 1: Spend some time in the garden. Get your hands dirty by planting seeds in a garden pot, then give your plants the water and sun they need to grow.

Time to build a garden in Minecraft. Craft a hoe out of any material you have available. Use the hoe to prepare the ground for your garden. Once you've used the hoe, pour water within a couple of blocks of your crop. For efficient use of crop watering, place the crops in rows with water in between.

■ **GAME MODE**

Creative

■ **APPROXIMATE TIME TO COMPLETE**

1 hour in Minecraft

■ **PLATFORMS**

PC/Mac, Consoles, PE

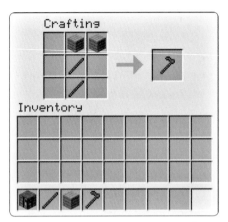

Fig. 1: Craft a hoe using sticks and wood, iron, stone, gold, or diamonds.

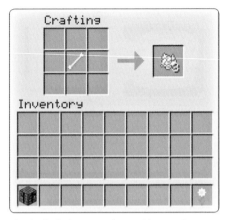

Fig. 2: Craft bone meal out of bones. One bone gives you three bone meals. Collect bones by killing skeletons.

1. Potatoes, wheat, carrots, melons, and pumpkins are food staples inside the game. Potatoes can be found at automatically generated NPC (non-player character) villages and, more rarely, by killing a zombie. An easy way to collect wheat seeds is to break tall grass.

2. Craft a hoe (fig. 1). The material you pick will be subject to wearing down as it is used. Hoes are only for preparing the ground for planting, so you won't need to craft many for a typical size garden. Right-click on the ground to prepare the soil for seeds.

Fig. 3: The left row has been fertilized with bone meal. The other two rows have been left to grow naturally.

3. Bone meal is your secret growth-hacking tool. Bone meal can be crafted from bones (fig. 2). With bone meal, most plants will grow almost instantly. Without bone meal, your crops will take a few day/night cycles to grow to the harvestable stage (fig. 3). Gather bones by killing skeletons.

4. Once the crop is fully grown, left-click on the plant to harvest. Beware: wandering mobs can destroy your garden. Protect your crops with walls of iron bars (fig. 4) or any other block that will keep mobs out.

MORE TO EXPLORE

Bone meal can also be used to create dye. Place bone meal in the center of the crafting table and a chunk of lapis lazuli to craft blue dye. Bone meal is an essential ingredient for crafting a white firework star.

Try your hand at automatic farming. You can use a piston system that drops water on the crops to automatically harvest all the plants.

The garden shown above was designed to promote rapid growth and easy access for harvesting. Because snow can hurt crops and freeze water, torches were placed nearby to keep them warm.

Fig. 4: Mobs can destroy your crops. You can prevent mobs from trampling them by placing iron bars to protect them.

QUEST 3

Timeless Architecture

Although gravity exists in Minecraft, it doesn't affect every block in the same way. While blocks such as dirt and stone seem to defy gravity, blocks of sand or gravel are often referred to as falling blocks. As an Architect and Designer, be sure to select the best blocks for the job. This quest is full of exciting opportunities to create and craft new designs.

PLACE
BADGE
HERE

Greek architecture is known for its strong columns
and high roofs. After the Romans conquered Greece,
they blended classic Greek elements with their own
arches and domes.

In this lab, you'll get to act like the Romans
through costume play, also called *cosplay,* a performance art where artists dress and act as characters.
You'll also create Roman-style, Greek-influenced
architecture in Minecraft.

Fig. 2: A classic
Roman laurel wreath.

Family Activity: Creative Cosplay

■ **APPROXIMATE TIME TO COMPLETE**
1 hour

■ **MATERIALS**
Long piece of fabric or flat bed sheet
(to make the toga)
Headband, real or artificial leaves,
and glue gun or white glue
(to make the laurel wreath crown)

The toga is a classic piece of ancient Roman fashion. It was reserved for Roman citizens. Roman slaves wore only a simple tunic, without a toga layered over it.

A laurel wreath represented Roman victory in war, and was worn by the emperor as a sign of his divinity. Creating your own laurel wreath will help you get into character.

Fig. 1: This girl is wearing a toga and carrying an *amphora,* a roman water jar.

1. Take the long piece of fabric and wrap it over one shoulder. The Romans typically wore a tunic made from linen under the toga. Wrap the toga behind your back and tie it up on your shoulder. The toga should cover one shoulder and most of your body (fig 1).

2. To craft a laurel wreath (fig. 2), collect some real or artificial leaves. Use a glue gun or white glue to attach the leaves onto a headpiece base, such as a headband.

MORE TO EXPLORE
To get in the Roman mood, watch the classic movie *Julius Caesar.* The 1953 classic is a great way to inspire your crafting, both in and out of the game.

 ONLINE RESOURCES
There are several different types of togas. Research them online and get inspired to create one that fits your personality.

In this part of the lab, we build Roman-inspired columns and a dome. The goal of building a dome is to create the sense of a large, open indoor space. When other players visit your dome, they'll be impressed because you've shaped your dome perfectly and decorated it with colorful blocks. It may help to sketch your design on paper before starting your build.

■ **GAME MODE**

Creative

■ **APPROXIMATE TIME TO COMPLETE**

2–3 hours in Minecraft

■ **PLATFORMS**

PC/Mac, Consoles, PE

1. Unlike most Minecraft builds, which typically start from the ground up, it's easiest to build a dome by starting with columns and working on top of them. We used chiseled quartz stone to build a column about thirty blocks high (fig. 1), but you can use blocks of any color. Build three more columns and arrange them in a square.

2. Begin adding layers of block to the tops of the columns to build up the dome (fig. 2).

GREEK AND ROMAN ARCHITECTURE

◀ The Romans were known for their use of arches in their architecture. One notable example is the Colosseum in Rome, Italy. Arches provide strong support in Minecraft builds, especially large ones.

▲ The Romans also built the Pantheon, which to this day is the largest unreinforced dome in the world.

▶ Built in the 400s BCE and dedicated as a temple to the Greek goddess Athena, the Parthenon happens to be 14 Minecraft blocks tall, 30 blocks long, and 19 blocks wide.

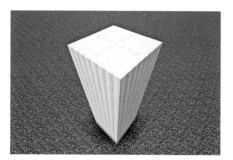

Fig. 1: Use thirty-block-high columns as the base for your dome build.

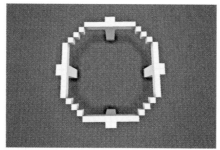

Fig. 2: The first layer of blocks has been added to the columns.

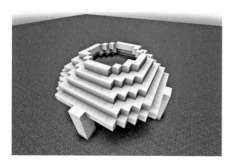

Fig. 3: Working toward the center, continue adding layers of blocks to build the dome into a half-sphere.

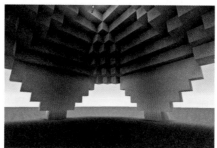

Fig. 4: You can also add blocks to the sides of the columns.

3. As you continue adding on sections of the dome, be aware of the space underneath it. The inside of the dome should be like half of a hollow sphere (fig. 3).

4. You can also add solid layers to the sides of the columns (fig. 4), or you can model your arches after a famous Roman building, like the Colosseum. Either way, you can always go back and break blocks that don't work with your design.

5. Decorate the inside of the dome with glowstone, torches, diamond, gold and any other fancy block. You might also use colored wood blocks to create a rainbow effect.

MORE TO EXPLORE

- The larger the build and farther away you view it, the rounder and smoother it will appear. Try it out by building a much larger dome and viewing it as far away as possible.
- It might be fun to build the Minecraft part of this lab while wearing the toga and laurel wreath you made in the family activity.

ONLINE RESOURCE

Plotz.co.uk is a great site to help you design rounded objects in Minecraft: *http://goo.gl/dUu8fk*.

Flying Machine

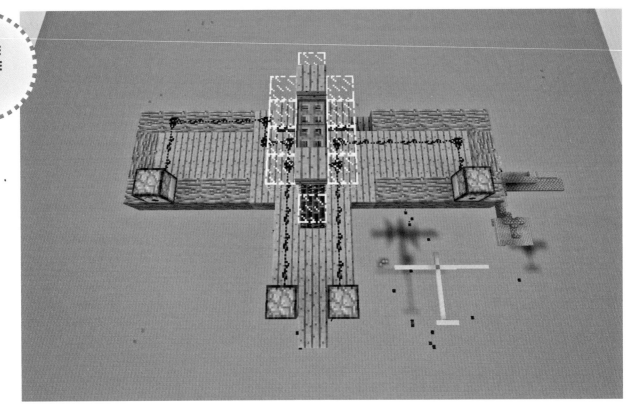

Paper airplanes have a long history that goes back to the manufacture of paper and the art of origami in China and perhaps Japan. Leonardo da Vinci wrote of a parchment aircraft and tested paper versions of his ornithopter, an aircraft that flew by flapping its wings like a bird.

In this lab, you'll fold and fly paper airplanes in the family activity, then let your imagination run wild while crafting airships inside of Minecraft.

You may be familiar with paper airplanes, such as the classic dart, condor, delta wing, bullet, and stealth bomber, or even experimentals like the flying ring. In this family activity you'll have the chance to craft a few paper airplanes for a fun family flying competition. Ready to put your imaginative flying designs to the test?

Family Activity: Paper Airplanes

- **APPROXIMATE TIME TO COMPLETE**
  30 minutes

- **MATERIALS**
  Several sheets of paper, 8-1/2 x 11 inches (21.6 x 27.9 cm)

1. Build several paper airplane models (see figs. 1-6).

2. Set the flying arena. It could be a hallway, sidewalk, or backyard. Set a line to throw behind and check that the wind is calm.

3. Try out these paper airplane challenges: longest distance, shortest distance, longest timed flight, shortest timed flight, wackiest flight, highest flight, and the near-miss flight. The winner of the near-miss flight challenge will have a plane that almost crashes yet continues its flight.

4. Once you've tried making and flying a classic paper airplane, try customizing by adding flaps, rudders, elevators, and weights to improve the design.

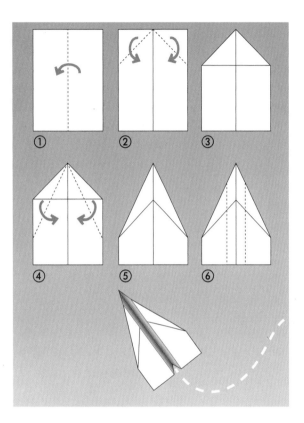

Fig. 1-6: Follow these simple steps to make basic paper planes, then let them fly!

ONLINE RESOURCE
There are hundreds of different types of paper airplanes that are ready to be put to the challenge. Check out this site for templates: *http://goo.gl/tBxJJ6.*

MORE TO EXPLORE
Takuo Toda holds the world record of 27.9 seconds for the longest time his paper airplane was in the air. Joe Ayoob holds the distance record of over 226 feet (69 m).

There are many different types of airships that have been crafted inside of Minecraft. Blimps, spaceships, airplanes, kites, helicopters, birds, magic carpets, and superheroes are just a few of the flying creations people have made inside of Minecraft.

■ **GAME MODE**

Creative

■ **APPROXIMATE TIME TO COMPLETE**

2–3 hours in Minecraft

■ **PLATFORMS**

PC/Mac, Consoles, PE

 ONLINE RESOURCE

Flying in Minecraft is possible with the Parachute Mod. Here's a link: *http://goo.gl/niat6n*

Fig. 1: With the column of any type of block you can build into the sky. This glider is almost ready for liftoff.

1. Build a column of blocks. Use any type of block to build to a height of your choice.

2. From the top of the column start building your airship. Build the bottom of the fuselage, then move on to the wings (fig. 1).

3. Break the column. Minecraft offers us a little bit of magic at this step. Once you've built the column, you can break the lower blocks while the rest float in the air. Your airship will have the appearance of floating (fig. 2).

4. Build more airships. A single airship is nice, but it's even cooler to have a fleet of ships. Imagine a favorite book, TV show, or movie as you create a fleet of custom airships. You're limited only by your imagination (figs. 3 and 4).

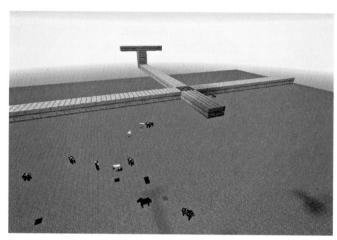

Fig. 2: There's a little magic in Minecraft. Even though you can place blocks in midair, you can build a tall structure and break the blocks below. This makes the build look like it's flying.

Fig. 3: A squadron of funky airships. The sky is the limit when it comes to building flying creations in Minecraft.

Fig. 4: This ship has been built with redstone-activated dispensers. Design and build an airship unlike any that's ever been crafted!

SHARE YOUR WORK

- The easiest way to share your airship is by taking a screenshot and publishing it online with the hashtag #minecrafterbook. Use a screen recording program to create a video tour and share it on YouTube.

- Using the mod MCedit, you can copy and paste schematics into your world. Schematics are builds that people have created and share online by allowing others to download and paste into their own games. Do a web search for "schematics airships Minecraft" and you'll find lots of great options.

- If you're ready for the next step, you can make and share a schematic of your airship.

The Architect

PLACE
BADGE
HERE

One of the most amazing aspects of Minecraft is the ability to easily design, build, tear down, and rebuild projects. Professional architects spend a lot of time designing a project before they ever see their designs built. In Minecraft, every player is an architect. Players plan, design, and iterate their builds with ease.

In this lab, you get a chance to experience building a castle in and out of the game. In the family activity, you'll build it out of sugar cubes. For building inspiration, choose a theme for your castle.

Castles have plenty of history that you can reference for inspiration for your build. We'll use sugar cubes for this family activity, but you're welcome to use any material you have available. Clay, cardboard, toothpicks, and even uncooked spaghetti are all great project materials.

Fig. 1: Gather the frosting, sugar cubes, and spreading stick.

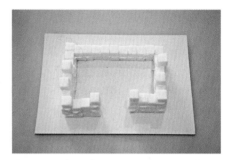

Fig. 2: Build the foundation of your castle on a piece of cardboard. Be sure to include an entrance.

■ **APPROXIMATE TIME TO COMPLETE**
1–2 hours

■ **MATERIALS**
Sugar cubes
Frosting
Cardboard
Spreading stick

Fig. 3: Continue building the walls higher.

Fig. 4: Once you've finished your castle, you can use it to create a make-believe world with made-up characters.

1. Gather the materials (fig. 1). You'll need plenty of sugar cubes (or other materials of your choice). If you're using sugar cubes, frosting works best as a glue; white glue can dissolve some of the sugar in the sugar cubes.

2. Build the foundation. Using a piece of cardboard as a temporary support is an easy way to build straight walls. Glue one sugar cube at a time and be sure to wipe up any excess frosting (fig. 2).

3. Every castle needs a tower. Here you can look out onto your land as well as station soldiers to defend the castle. Add extra sugar cubes to build the tower taller than the rest of the castle (fig. 3).

4. Castle towers used parapets, crenellations, machicolations, arrow loops, and other designs to protect soldiers as they defended the castle (fig. 4).

5. You can also design and build a portcullis, the heavy gate that blocks entry into the castle. You can always add a working drawbridge, or even a moat, for extra flair. If you're adding rooms to your build, add them before you add a roof.

MORE TO EXPLORE
Windsor Castle, the oldest still-occupied castle in Europe, is in the English county of Berkshire.

In this Minecraft build, you get to claim your land and build a castle. Research castles to find your inspiration.

■ **GAME MODE**
Creative

■ **APPROXIMATE TIME TO COMPLETE**
2–3 hours in Minecraft

■ **PLATFORMS**
PC/Mac, Consoles, PE

1. **Design your castle. Some builders start by drawing out their build on paper, while others go directly into the game to start building.**

2. **Build the first wall, which should be the front of the castle. From there you can gauge how big the remaining walls should be. Plan for a large enough opening for your entrance portcullis. If you build the walls five blocks thick, then you'll have space on top of the wall for soldiers to scan the horizon for potential threats (fig. 1).**

3. **Build the remaining walls. Some castles have four walls, while others have five or more. Build the remaining castle walls to your design specifications.**

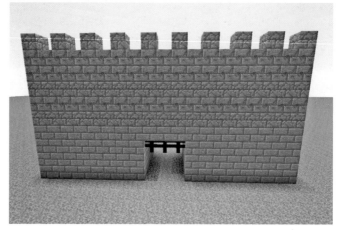

Fig. 1: The front wall is the best place to start your castle.

4. **Design and build the interior. Build rooms inside the towers, and perhaps even a loft. Castles are like mini cities inside. All castles need a steady supply of food. When building your castle garden, be sure to make a water source nearby. Tip: Use bone meal to make the crops grow extra fast (see page 57). Use wooden fence blocks to protect your gardens and create animal pens, then spawn your favorite animals (figs. 2 and 3). Watch out— the chickens can fly.**

5. **Create a portcullis. Nether bricks look great as a portcullis. You can build one nether brick on top of another to fill the opening to your castle (fig. 4).**

 ONLINE RESOURCES

There are Minecraft blueprints online for all types of castles, including Hogwarts from J.K. Rowling's *Harry Potter*. Here's a link to a video tour of an incredible Minecraft version of Hogwarts castle:
https://youtu.be/1ftVC8vNWAY

Fig. 2: Use fence blocks to create pens for the castle's animals.

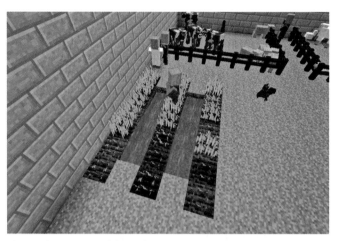

Fig. 3: Plant your castle's gardens near a water source.

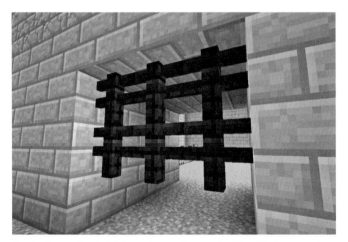

Fig. 4: Use nether brick fence to create a portcullis—the heavy gate that drops down to block intruders—with a dark look.

MORE TO EXPLORE

Work with redstone to design a working drawbridge. Keep in mind that your drawbridge may not work in the traditional manner.

 SHARE YOUR WORK

Once your castle is complete, share it with other players by inviting them to play capture the flag. Play in survival mode and make sure the tools players have are agreed upon. We suggest wooden tools because the game will last longer. The winner grabs the flag from the opponent and returns it to his or her castle.

Built to Scale

Scale is a representation of dimensions. Architects and engineers use scale regularly as an accurate way of changing the size of objects like homes.

In the family activity in this lab, you'll measure and draw a scale version of your home or room. In the game activity, you will recreate your home or room in varying scales. Try your hand at creating a smaller version of your home and a 1:1 scale where the measurements of your home are the same in and out of the game.

Family Activity: Sketch a Scale Drawing

Learn about measurements and creating scale drawings as you sketch a scale drawing of a room in your home.

▦ APPROXIMATE TIME TO COMPLETE
1 hour

▦ MATERIALS
Measuring tape
Pencil
Note paper
Graph paper (see page 139)

1. **Dig out a measuring tape, as you are going to measure your home or room. You can pick a room or your entire home. Go around with the measuring tape to find the length of each wall. Start by measuring the longest room or hallway. Jot down the measurements on the piece of paper (fig. 1).**

2. **As you take measurements, draw an outline of the home or room. To draw to scale, you'll need to convert your measurements to a smaller size. An example is to make 1 foot equal to 1 inch. So, if your longest wall is 15 feet long, you'll draw a 15-inch line. Or, every 10 cm could be equal to 1 cm. (A 457 cm wall would be drawn as 45.7 cm.) Using graph paper will help you get accurate drawings (fig. 2).**

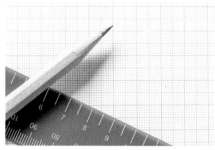

Fig. 1: With just a few tools you can measure your home or room. Jot down your measurements for easy reference during your build.

Fig. 2: As you take measurements, create an outline drawing of your home or room.

3. **Measure the length and width of furniture, such as couches, chairs, and beds. Be sure to include lighting, as you'll want to include appropriate lighting in your Minecraft build.**

MORE TO EXPLORE
Scale in art and design is often associated with proportion. Scale is the size of one object in relation to another, while proportion is the size of parts of an object in relation to the whole. The colorful snail sculptures below represent larger-than-life scale, even though all the snails are in proportion to each other. The Great Wall of China (bottom) is massive in scale as it is thousands of miles long, though in proportion to the Chinese countryside it seems small.

Craft your scale drawing inside of Minecraft using any block material.

▪ **GAME MODE**
Creative

▪ **APPROXIMATE TIME TO COMPLETE**
2–3 hours in Minecraft

▪ **PLATFORMS**
PC/Mac, Consoles, PE

1. **Start by converting 1 foot (30.5 cm) of home to 1 block. Technically, a block is a cubic meter. We are starting with a scale version before we get to the 1:1 size of the home or room (fig. 1).**

2. **Using the 1 foot (30.5 cm) equals 1 block scale, build the foundation of your home (fig. 2).**

3. **Carefully go through the build and add walls and rooms based on their scale measurements. Once the walls are up, you'll be able to build a roof that looks like the one on your house (fig. 3).**

Fig. 1: Blocks in Minecraft are 1 meter cubed. Each arrow is 1 meter long.

4. **Add lighting, couches, beds, tables, chairs, and other decorative items and details (fig. 4).**

5. **Create a scale landscape around your home. Add new features to make your landscape and home the place of your dreams. Minecraft is great at visualizing dreams.**

ONLINE RESOURCES

One of the incredible scale models built in Minecraft is the starship USS *Enterprise*. The Taj Mahal as well as many cities and countries have also been recreated inside Minecraft. You can use Google Maps to measure a famous building and build a scale replica. Once you're on the map, right-click to see the "measure" option. Click on the map and a measurement line will appear. Consider measuring and building a scale model of the Eiffel Tower. Here's a link to the Google map with measurements: *https://goo.gl/GflClT*

Fig. 2: Start by building your house's foundation.

SHARE YOUR WORK

Share your build with the world by taking screenshots of your Minecraft home. Publish it online and use the hashtag *#minecrafterbook* when sharing.

Fig. 3: Add a roof once you've built the walls.

Fig. 4: The interior of this simple house includes chairs, a couch, and bookshelves.

The Arts

In this quest, explore blocks of various colors, textures, and styles to create museum space and fill it with paintings, sculpture, music, and a stage for performances.

Creating Figures

In the game, you and your family will work together to design a museum or cultural center that you can use for the entire quest. Throughout the space, you'll need enough room for statues on pedestals, paintings in frames, a stage for performance, and a hall for music.

In the family activity, you'll create a model of your character, or that of a favorite Minecraft player, to place in your museum. Parents may want to create a custom skin for their character prior to beginning.

Family Activity: Make a Foldable 3-D Paper Character

For this hands-on activity, everyone will be creating their own 3-D version of their character, or that of a favorite Minecraft personality, using the website pixelpapercraft.com.

▓ **APPROXIMATE TIME TO COMPLETE**
1–2 hours

▓ **MATERIALS**
Access to a color printer
Scissors and glue
Minecraft username for each
  character you wish to recreate

1. **Visit pixelpapercraft.com and choose "Print" from the menu options.**

2. **Select "Print," then "Generators." Choose "Minecraft Character," click "Skin," and enter your Minecraft username. You'll see a deconstructed, printable image of your Minecraft character(fig. 1).**

3. **Print out the image and use scissors and glue to cut out and assemble the body parts (fig. 2).**

4. **Just for fun, you can also cut out and assemble the print version of one of our Minecraft characters (see page 135).**

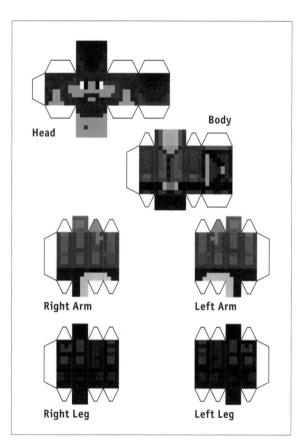

Head Body

Right Arm Left Arm

Right Leg Left Leg

Fig. 1: Print out a foldable model of your Minecraft character. This one appears full size on page 135.

Fig. 2: Cut out and glue the pieces together to create a 3-D paper character.

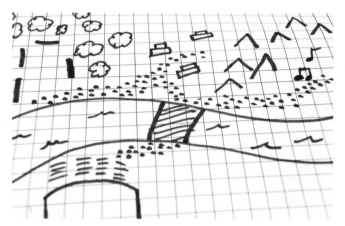

Fig. 1: Design your museum on paper first. You'll need four exhibit spaces for this quest.

Fig. 2: Create an attractive pedestal. You'll need an 8x4 space to support the legs.

Your challenge is in two parts. First, design the layout for a museum with indoor and outdoor space where you can display your creations. Second, sculpt your character on top of a pedestal for all to admire.

■ **GAME MODE**

Creative

■ **APPROXIMATE TIME TO COMPLETE**

2–3 hours in Minecraft

■ **PLATFORMS**

PC/Mac, Consoles, PE

1. **Plan and then build the museum space and the pedestals you'll use to display your completed statues. Graph paper (see page 139) will be useful to designate areas of the museum. Future labs in this quest will ask you to add spaces within your museum to display paintings as well as locations for music and dramatic performance (fig. 1).**

2. **Locate a suitable biome in your Minecraft world that works best with your design. Perhaps your museum might hover in the sky or float on the ocean. Consider the location of the rising and setting sun, water features, and especially pretty views before building. Flatten out any area that needs it, lay out your floor plan, and build your pedestals (fig. 2).**

ONLINE RESOURCES

The Tate Modern Museum in London commissioned Minecraft builders and artists to create amazing interactive Minecraft worlds based on works of art in their collection. You can download these worlds for free by visiting: *http://goo.gl/Nvg2DB*

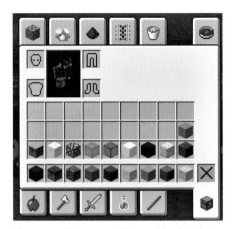

Fig. 3: Load up your toolbar and backpack with appropriate colors and textures.

Fig. 4: Build your sculpture from the ground up.

Fig. 5: Use glowstone to light up pathways and your sculpture at night.

3. Determine the size of each sculpture based on skill level. Beginners may wish to sculpt a bust of the head while more advanced players should recreate the entire body.

4. Use the 3-D character you created in the family activity as a model and prepare your palette. Choose blocks that closely match your character's colors and add them to your toolbar and backpack for quick access (fig. 3).

5. Sculpt your character from the ground up to eliminate mistakes later (fig. 4).

6. Add lighting (glowstone) to illuminate your masterpiece at night (fig. 5). Create walkways and viewing platforms between each sculpture.

SHARE YOUR WORK

Share this lab online or in print by creating a collage combining images taken of your 3D characters with your Minecraft build. Be sure to include multiple angles and images of your work taken at night and caption each image. Use the hashtag #minecrafterbook when sharing.

I Hear Music

PLACE
BADGE
HERE

In the first lab of this quest, you created a museum space to showcase the four labs you will be completing. You also created sculptures of your favorite Minecraft characters. Now it's time to expand your museum by adding a music hall!

In this lab, you'll be learning how to use note blocks in Minecraft to create musical notes. In the family activity, you'll first recreate a famous tune for practice, then each player will create a five-note (or more) tune of his or her own. Finally, everyone will link their tunes together with redstone to create a song and place it in your museum.

Family Activity: Matchbox Guitar

- **APPROXIMATE TIME TO COMPLETE**

  1 hour

- **MATERIALS (for 1 guitar; make 1 per family member)**

  An empty matchbox

  Tape

  Several rubber bands

  A pencil

1. Open the empty matchbox slightly and apply tape to the underside to keep it open. You'll use the open side to make your guitar (fig. 1).

2. Stretch and equally space three rubber bands over the length of the matchbox. If using a small matchbox, use one rubber band and twist it twice on the back. The bands need to run parallel on the top of the box (fig. 2).

3. Insert the pencil under the rubber bands and at an angle across the top of the box (fig. 3). The pencil will act as a bridge and let you adjust the pitch of each note.

4. Slide the pencil up and down the box and pluck each rubber band until you find a pleasant combination of notes. Each person should create an instrument that produces different notes.

5. Create a simple tune by plucking each band and combining each person's instrument in a sequence (fig 4).

Fig. 1: Apply tape to the sides of the open matchbox to prevent it from closing.

Fig. 2: Space three rubber bands out equally.

Fig. 3: Inserting the pencil at different angles will produce different notes.

Fig. 4: Take turns plucking notes to compose a tune.

In this part of the lab, you'll be recreating one of the most recognizable tunes in history—the opening of Beethoven's 5th Symphony. Dah-Dah-Dah-DUH . . .

Read the sidebar Lab Prep (right) before you begin.

- **GAME MODE**
  Creative

- **APPROXIMATE TIME TO COMPLETE**
  2–3 hours

- **PLATFORMS**
  PC/Mac, Consoles

1. **Place four note blocks in a row, one space apart from each other. Beginning with the first block, place one repeater between it and the next block. Repeat until you have placed three repeaters. Right-click on each repeater twice to slow the signal traveling between each block (fig. 1).**

2. **Now connect the first block to a button or pressure plate using redstone and tune each block. The notes you need are G-G-G-*Eb* (E flat). For each of the first three blocks, click thirteen times for G and for the last block, click ten times for E*b*. Play your first composition by activating the pressure plate or button (figs. 2–5).**

Fig. 1: Adjust the repeater switches to slow the signal passing through them.

Fig. 2: Adjust the pitch of the first block by clicking thirteen times.

Fig. 3: The second block should also be tuned thirteen times.

LAB PREP

Here are some things to know before starting the Minecraft part of the lab:

- You'll be using redstone repeaters in this lab. When placed, a repeater delays the signal traveling through the repeater by 0.1 second. You can adjust any repeater to slow a signal by up to 0.4 second. Connect repeaters in a sequence to delay the signal even longer.
- Note blocks are available in creative mode or through crafting in survival mode by combining eight wood planks with redstone.
- You can replicate five different musical instruments using note blocks.
- Right-clicking on the note block more than once increases the pitch of the note up to twenty-four times before resetting.
- Use redstone to connect note blocks. There's no limit to the number of blocks you can connect together. Activate note blocks using a lever, button, or pressure plate.

3. Now it is time to compose your own tune in the Minecraft Museum you created in the first lab of this quest. Use the information in steps 1 and 2 to set up your note blocks. This time you will need at least five. Experiment with different instruments by placing wood, glass, stone, or sand blocks beneath each note block and adjusting the pitch. Use one or more repeaters between blocks to slow the tempo.

4. When everyone is finished with his or her individual tune, merge them together to create a melody. There are at least two options for doing this. The easiest is to begin with the first tune and then ask everyone to attach his or her tune in one long sequence (fig. 6).

5. A more challenging way is to create an array of blocks side by side. See the main image on page 82, which shows a final array of note blocks in an outdoor symphony hall. Can you think of a creative way to build your array in your museum?

SHARE YOUR WORK

Share your collaborative creation by making a short video and posting it to YouTube. Don't forget to give credit to everyone who helped create the melody and use the hashtag *#minecrafterbook* when sharing.

Fig. 4: Adjust the third block thirteen times as well.

Fig. 5: The final block in the sequence needs to be clicked ten times to create an E♭.

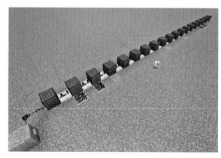

Fig. 6: To create a long sequence of notes, place note blocks on top of other common blocks. For illustration purposes, blocks have been placed both under and adjacent to each note block.

MORE TO EXPLORE

Getting notes to play one at a time is straightforward, but in order to have notes play over other notes, you need to think 3-D. To save space, stack note blocks vertically. You will need to think creatively here because each note block must have at least one block of air above it to play.

ONLINE RESOURCES

- Watch this video for one way to play multiple notes at a time: *https://goo.gl/1pYPsh*
- There are many dedicated note block composers on YouTube, and one of the best is ValcanGaming. Perhaps he has recreated a favorite song of yours? Check it out here: *https://goo.gl/OTj5m8*

In this lab, you'll first recreate a favorite scene from a book or story using Minecraft shadow puppets in the family activity. Then you'll take what you've learned and recreate that same scene or a new one inside your Minecraft museum. It's a chance for the whole family to perform under the bright glowstone lights on stage!

 ONLINE RESOURCES
- Read about the legend of *The Butterfly Lovers* here: *https://goo.gl/YPX8Rc*
- For help making a shadow puppet, watch this video created by a professional puppeteer: *https://goo.gl/4RVGhI*

Family Activity: Shadow Puppets

To begin this lab, you'll make shadow puppets and perform a scene from a favorite story. Shadow plays have a long tradition in China and Southeast Asia. We were inspired by the traditional Chinese story of *The Butterfly Lovers*, considered to be one of China's great folktales. Like Shakespeare's *Romeo and Juliet*, the legend of *The Butterfly Lovers* is about two tragic lovers.

Fig. 1: Sketch your character before cutting it out. Use the template on page 137 to make a butterfly.

Fig. 2: Attach each puppet to a stick with tape.

■ **APPROXIMATE TIME TO COMPLETE**
  1–2 hours

■ **MATERIALS**
  A short story with enough characters for each family member
  Construction paper in a dark color, such as black or brown
  Scissors
  Tape
  Long sticks
  Focused light source, such as a small spot lamp or bright flashlight

Fig. 3: Perform your play by casting your puppets' shadows onto a wall or other surface.

1. Everyone will create a character from the scene you've selected. Sketch the outline of the character on the black construction paper. Use Minecraft-inspired mobs and characters, or create original puppets to tell your story. We created butterflies to represent our characters (fig. 1). See page 137 for a full-size template.

2. Cut out each character and tape it to the long stick to make it come alive (fig. 2).

3. Traditionally, shadow plays involve a thin, light-colored fabric on which the puppeteers project their puppets' shadows from behind. You'll need to hang a sheet if you wish to perform your play this way; otherwise, you can project your story from the front onto a blank wall using a focused light source (fig. 3).

Using Minecraft to animate short stories is widely popular. Kids and adults are producing and sharing thousands of hours of original stories they create in Minecraft on YouTube. In this part of the lab, you'll take a scene from a story or movie that you like, build replica sets, write dialogue, perform, and record the scene before posting it on YouTube.

Before you start, take a few moments to watch the video by YouTuber Adam Clarke, a.k.a. Wizard Keen, called *When Stampy Came to Tea*, a retelling of the story *When Tiger Came to Tea* by Judith Kerr (see the link opposite).

■ **GAME MODE**
Creative

■ **APPROXIMATE TIME TO COMPLETE**
2–3 hours in Minecraft

■ **PLATFORMS**
PC/Mac, Xbox, PlayStation, PE

Fig. 1: Using a storyboard lets you see what each scene will look like before you film it.

Fig. 2: Create a stage for your performance and dress it with items from your inventory.

1. **Decide on a short scene to recreate. It should be under five minutes. Before filming any scenes of a movie, directors draw a quick and simple sketch of what they want each scene to look like using paper (fig. 1). A movie where the camera angle never changes can be boring. By changing the position of your camera, your viewers will get a different perspective of the action.**

2. **Now that you know what you need your set to look like, it's time to build it into your museum complex. Consider building it outdoors and turning it into a proper theater, but not too far away from the music hall and sculpture garden (fig. 2). If you need help, check out the link found opposite to get a behind-the-scenes look at *When Stampy Came to Tea*.**

3. **Write the dialogue for each character in the scene and have each player practice reading aloud. Your script might look something like this:**

Villager: Have you been to our village before, Witch Claire? It seems I recognize you.

Witch: Thank you for asking me to tea. Even though I have flown by often, I've never actually visited this village before.

Villager: Perhaps we met somewhere else. Have you ever been to Mushroom Park near Middlebury? I am a regular visitor. I collect mushrooms there for my stew.

Fig. 3: Rehearse to determine your camera angles.

ONLINE RESOURCES

- Adam Clarke is a very talented Minecraft YouTuber. To see his movie *When Stampy Came to Tea*, check out this link: *https://goo.gl/BEssTn*
- After Adam finished producing *When Stampy Came to Tea*, he wanted to share how he created the video in hopes of inspiring others to do the same. To learn how to tell a story using Minecraft, watch his video: *https://goo.gl/2PYeKp*

Fig. 4: Dig yourself a hole and hop in it to get a more interesting camera angle.

4. Rehearse the scene with all the actors and determine the camera angles you'll use (fig. 3).

5. It's time to film the scene (fig. 4). Refer to page 20 for tips on filming or screencasting your video.

6. When you've completed your video, it may need a bit of editing. If that's the case, you can edit it after you upload to your YouTube channel. Use the video editor (see page 18) to combine your scenes, add music and titles, and publish your masterpiece.

MORE TO EXPLORE
For players looking for a bit more of a challenge, consider these options:
- Film multiple scenes.
- Design scenes that involve advanced redstone use.
- Create an action adventure with special effects and TNT explosions.
- Add custom skins for costumes, and try different voices or accents.

SHARE YOUR WORK
Post your completed video on your YouTube channel and share it online using the hashtag *#minecrafterbook*

LAB
16

The Art of the Block

Minecraft's blocky look, patterns, and textures have inspired players of all ages to create amazing works of "pixel art."

In the family activity portion of this lab, you'll use graph paper to make a pixel art masterpiece. Then you'll use the suggested resources to create one or more pixel art canvases to hang in your Minecraft Museum and conclude Quest 4.

Family Activity: Pixel Art Design

Creating art by replacing computer pixels with blocks is a very popular activity in the Minecraft community. To begin this lab, each family member will design a piece of pixel art.

■ **APPROXIMATE TIME TO COMPLETE**
1 hour

■ **MATERIALS**
Graph paper (see page 139)
Colored pencils, crayons, or markers

Fig. 1: Use colored pencils to sketch your Minecraft pixel art on graph paper.

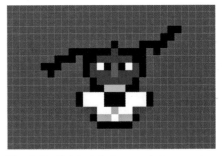
Fig. 2: Our finished design, ready to recreate for our Minecraft museum.

1. Select an image you would like to recreate in Minecraft. If you don't know what to draw, do a web image search for "8 bit art" and find an image you like, or visit the Minecraft PixelArt website (see Online Resource, below, left) for examples and inspiration.

2. Using graph paper and colored pencils, crayons, or markers, color in each box to create an original design (fig. 1). We designed a funky alien dog (fig. 2).

ONLINE RESOURCE
The Minecraft PixelArt website has many examples and lots of inspiration to get you started: *http://goo.gl/gCPbOE*

MORE TO EXPLORE
Pablo Picasso (1881-1973) was an influential Spanish artist who created many art styles and techniques. One of the techniques he helped develop was cubism, which breaks the subject of an artwork down into abstract shapes that show the subject from more than one point of view. Minecraft's pixelated look is in some ways similar to cubism because it breaks objects and figures down into simple block shapes.

Minecraft Play: Paint a Picture with Blocks

■ **GAME MODE**
Creative

■ **APPROXIMATE TIME TO COMPLETE**
2–3 hours in Minecraft

■ **PLATFORMS**
PC/Mac, Consoles, PE

1. Determine a location in your museum to "paint" your masterpiece. Will you view your gallery from above? On a platform? If so, you can create your work of art on a flat space near the viewing area. Alternatively, you can choose to have your masterpiece hover in the air. To do this, you'll need to build a temporary pillar in the air to which you can attach the bottom row of blocks (fig. 1).

2. Search for blocks that match or are similar to the colors in the image you created in the family activity part of this lab. Drag potentially useful blocks onto your toolbar and into your backpack. If you need more storage, place a chest atop a pillar near your canvas and fill it with more blocks as needed (fig. 2).

Fig. 1: To place blocks in midair, first build a tall pillar, place your bottom row of blocks atop it, then remove the pillar.

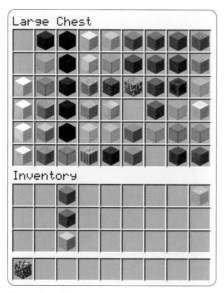

Fig. 2: Your inventory and backpack can hold dozens of blocks. If you need more space, place a storage chest near your painting as you work.

3. It's often easiest to begin with the center or most difficult section of the image and work your way out. Take your time here and look for symmetry on each side, which will make placing later blocks easier (fig. 3). Don't bite off more than you can chew. Work as a team if you want to create something larger.

4. Display each pixel art painting in a frame within your gallery. Explore the different Minecraft blocks until you find one or more that you would like to use as a frame. Consider different colors and textures and add glowstone blocks to the edges of your frame for backlighting at night (fig. 4).

ONLINE RESOURCE
Websites like printcraft.org let you print your Minecraft creations using a 3-D printer. Did you make something in this quest that you are really proud of? Print it!

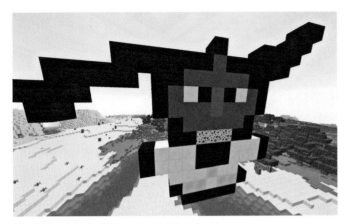

Fig. 3: Carefully build your image block by block.

MORE TO EXPLORE

Add another level to this challenge by creating pixel art from an original digital photograph. Open your photograph using an image editor on your computer and adjust the image size to seventy-two pixels wide. Zoom in until the pixels are a comfortable size for viewing. Artwork created from photographs contain many more pixels than 8-bit images do, and, therefore, it needs to be viewed from farther away to be recognizable.

Fig. 4: Add a frame, then fill in the gaps around your image. Fly back a few blocks and admire everyone's work.

SHARE YOUR WORK

Share your pixel art with the world by taking screenshots of your family artwork and creating a "gallery walk" slideshow. Publish it online and use the hashtag *#minecrafterbook* when sharing.

Game Design

Use Minecraft to create three games that each family member can take part in and then link them together in a challenging timed course with an explosive conclusion.

Players have been using the mechanics of Minecraft to craft highly creative and interactive games ever since the game first came out. This is the first of three labs that ask your team to work collaboratively to create arcade- or carnival-style games using Minecraft. In the family activity, you'll create a target shooting game using a bow and arrows you craft from cotton swabs and Popsicle sticks, then you'll build a mini archery game in Minecraft.

Family Activity: Mini Bow and Arrows

This mini bow and arrow set is inspired by a project on the Brooding Hen blog (*http://goo.gl/P4Tor*). After everyone creates his or her own set, it's off to the range to see who the best shot is.

■ **APPROXIMATE TIME TO COMPLETE**

1¹/₂–2 hours

■ **MATERIALS**

Sharp knife
Popsicle sticks
Dental floss
Scissors
Cotton swabs

1. Using the knife, cut four notches near the ends of the Popsicle stick, two on each end, directly opposite one another (fig. 1).

2. Submerge the Popsicle stick in water for at least an hour to make it pliable (fig. 2).

3. Wrap and tie the dental floss tightly first around two notches at one end of the stick. Carefully pull the floss taut, bending the stick in the process to create a bow shape. Tie the floss off on the notches at the opposite end of the stick (fig. 3).

Fig. 1: Cut out two notches at both ends of the Popsicle stick.

Fig. 2: Soak the stick in water for at least an hour.

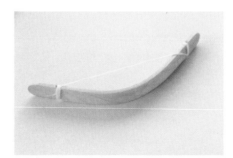

Fig. 3: Tie the dental floss around the notches on one end of the stick, pull it to bend the stick into a bow shape, then tie it off at the other end.

Fig. 4: Snip off one end of the cotton swab to make an arrow.

4. Snip off one end of the cotton swab to create an arrow (fig. 4). Test out your bow.

5. Load the arrow and fire away at a target or bowl and determine who the best shot in the family is.

Before you begin this part of the lab, find a location in Minecraft that meets the following criteria so you can build out the three games in this quest:

- A relatively flat area to host your archery tournament with good line of sight

- An open area where you can build steps high into the sky

- A sloping area or mountain nearby, to be used in creating a boat race through the rapids

The mini archery game you build as a team should have at least three different types of challenges based on the experience levels of the participants. For example, one or more might involve redstone and a scoring system. Another might be a simple series of targets set up at different ranges. Yet another could involve shooting mobs in the wild, in a gallery, or in another enclosed area. See the list at right for tips on using a bow and arrow in-game.

■ **GAME MODE**
Creative and Survival

■ **APPROXIMATE TIME TO COMPLETE**
1–2 hours in Minecraft

■ **PLATFORMS**
PC/Mac, Consoles, PE

1. **It's time to determine the kind of targets you'll be shooting. Stationary objects such as blocks, moving targets attached to items like sticky pistons or minecarts, or even random mobs provide good sport. In the example for this lab, we've set up three stations.**

   • **Activate the redstone lamp by hitting the wooden button with an arrow (fig. 1).**

   • **Collect points by hitting the center of each target (fig. 2).**

   • **Shoot at a redstone-powered chicken shooting gallery (fig. 3).**

MINECRAFT ARCHERY

- To launch an arrow from your inventory or when in creative mode, pull the bow back by holding the right-click button down until the string is all the way back and then release.

- Gravity affects arrows, so aim high if your target is far away.

- The maximum distance covered by an arrow is 120 blocks.

- You can pick up and reuse arrows shot by other players, but not arrows shot by skeletons.

- Use the flame enchantment to create flaming arrows that can blow up TNT.

- Arrows released at maximum bow tension cause the most damage.

- You can only move around at sneak speed if you have the bowstring pulled back.

- If crafting arrows in survival mode, you'll need flint, a stick, and a feather.

ONLINE RESOURCES
Mini games are one of the fastest growing areas for Minecraft builders, with new games coming out all the time. In the multiplayer Hot Potato, one player randomly receives a potato with a lit fuse and must pass it along to another player before it explodes. You can discover more and download a version by following this link: *http://goo.gl/FeTnBQ*

Fig. 1: Place a wooden button on a redstone lamp. Striking the button with an arrow will turn the lamp on, indicating an accurate shot.

Fig. 2: Set up target blocks at various distances and heights to test competitors' skills.

Fig. 3: As an extra challenge, create a redstone-activated shooting gallery.

2. Determine how your game will end. What will players need to do to be successful? Consider the following:

  • Can there be only one winner?

  • Is your game better if played with partners or in larger teams?

  • Will you limit the number of arrows each player shoots?

  • Will you time the game?

  • Will there be any bonus point opportunities?

3. Now build your mini game together and play test it along the way. Need a few ideas to help get you started? See the suggestions at right.

SHARE YOUR WORK

Save this as a world file and post it for download on your blog or website. Don't forget to provide a write-up with the directions and tips for winning. Credit everyone who helped create the game and use the hashtag *#minecrafterbook* when sharing online.

STARTER SUGGESTIONS

■ Make players craft their materials or use dispensers to issue arrows.

■ To make it more difficult, set one of your challenges atop a steep hill and require players to make high arcing shots.

■ Build the world in creative mode and play in survival mode, where shooting mobs earn bonus points.

■ Use paintings for targets—they'll disappear when hit.

■ Challenge players to shoot while riding a horse or pig, or have them ride a minecart through each station.

MORE TO EXPLORE

More advanced players can research how to set up a scoreboard system and a clock for this quest to easily track each player's score.

Parkour is a mini game that challenges players to complete an obstacle course as quickly as possible based on a popular French military fitness training exercise. Players use skills developed through playing Minecraft to leap, run, bounce, and sneak their way up, over, and through various obstacles designed to impede their progress.

In the family activity, you'll be using elements of Minecraft mechanics to design and build a parkour game collaboratively. In Minecraft, you'll be creating a parkour course, which should be built somewhere near the archery challenge you built in Lab 17.

Family Activity: Obstacle Course

It's time to get outside and breathe in the fresh air. You will be making an obstacle course somewhere outside your home or at a park using a few common items you may have. Your challenge is to create an obstacle course that everyone in the family can complete—with or without a little extra help.

▓ **APPROXIMATE TIME TO COMPLETE**

1–2 hours

▓ **MATERIALS**

Toy hoops

Buckets

Cones

Pool noodles

Rubber balls

Sports equipment

String or rope

Empty milk cartons or water bottles

Balloons

Chalk

Ladder

Brooms

1. **Discuss obstacle ideas and make a list of materials you'll need. You should create at least three challenges that each participant must complete to win. See the photos above and at right and the list far right for ideas.**

2. **Now set up your obstacle course challenge in an open location and let everyone have a go (figs. 1-3)!**

Fig. 1: Plastic hoops are great for ring toss, and are also good for targets and hopscotch.

Fig. 2: Get out your bikes and set up a challenging course.

Fig. 3: Is there a golfer (or mini golfer) on your team? Create one or more fun putting holes in your backyard.

OTHER OBSTACLE COURSE IDEAS

- Pool noodles have multiple uses: for example, as targets, spears, or posts.
- Set up buckets as obstacles, or use them to carry water or other items over a set distance.
- In order to advance, players must put on and take off a pile of old clothes.
- Create a challenge to complete with a blindfold.
- Build a tall tower that doesn't fall over using a pile of oddly shaped wood scraps.

Parkour is an immensely popular Minecraft mini game with multiple variations. Each person on the build team should be responsible for completing one part of the course you create. The object is simple: complete the course. But along the way you'll discover several challenges that you must overcome. Some require you to perfect your running and leaping skills. For others you'll need to make quick judgments and have perfect timing. You're likely to fail multiple times while attempting to complete the course, and that's half the fun! You may even die in the process if you play in survival mode, but don't worry—you'll respawn again and can have another go. See the list at right for common elements of parkour.

■ **GAME MODE**
  Build in Creative, Play in Survival

■ **APPROXIMATE TIME TO COMPLETE**
  3–4 hours together in Minecraft

■ **PLATFORMS**
  PC/Mac, Consoles, PE

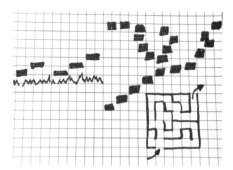

Fig. 1: Creating a list of blocks and challenging elements ahead of time will ensure that the course does not repeat.

1. Use a large sheet of white paper or graph paper to lay out your course. Each section of the course must be challenging yet passable after a few attempts. Make a list of the different blocks and elements used in each section so no one repeats an element (fig. 1).

2. As you build out your section, don't forget to provide a smooth transition from and to the previous and upcoming sections.

3. As you create your section, pause after a few blocks, back up a bit, and attempt to complete that section as if you were a player. If you can't get by the obstacle, modify your design and test it again (fig. 2). See the list opposite for some course ideas.

PARKOUR ESSENTIALS

A parkour course consists of a series of connected challenges.

- Players leap, run, and jump their way over blocks as quickly as possible. These are some basic rules and elements to the game in Minecraft.

- Falling from blocks inflicts damage to players. The higher your fall, the greater the damage. Leaping over lava pits is especially scary. Use water or sponges to soften a fall.

- Players taking too much damage die and respawn where they last appeared.

- The blocks that are most often used include slabs, stairs, ladders, and fences.

- Use a bit of glowstone to light the way in dark spaces.

MINECRAFT PARKOUR COURSE DESIGN IDEAS

- Connect a series of blocks and slabs in the air.
- Incorporate buildings or other structures into the course.
- Design a section to play inside a building.
- Create a dimly lit space and populate it with mobs.
- Have players fall through the course, landing on blocks along the way.
- Ladders will help players cling to a wall and can be used in short, interrupted segments.
- Provide multiple options and direction changes.

Fig. 2: Try out your course segment as you build it. You might discover sections that are too hard for all players to accomplish.

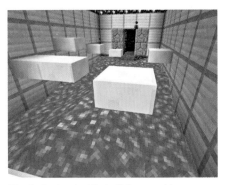

Fig. 3: Racing inside buildings and between floors is fun.

SHARE YOUR WORK

Share this map with your friends and record their experiences as they try to complete your course. Post the video on your YouTube channel and use the hashtag *#minecrafterbook* when sharing online.

MORE TO EXPLORE

Design your parkour course as a team challenge and use redstone and command blocks throughout. Set up a scoreboard system to record the number of deaths.

ONLINE RESOURCES

- Parkour maps are among the most popular downloaded maps for Minecraft. To find hundreds of maps ready to download, check out: minecraftmaps.com.
- To see an example of a fun parkour map, watch this video by Stampy: *http://goo.gl/s9Ptaa*

The final mini game you'll create for this quest will be a boat race between two or more competitors. In the family activity, everyone will create and decorate his or her own cork boat and race it across a body of water, then you'll build the course and have the race in Minecraft. Design a course full of obstacles like rapids, waterfalls, and slalom gates, which players must find their way around as quickly as possible.

Family Activity: Cork Sailboats

In this nautical adventure, you'll each design and create your own cork sailboat and race it around a challenging watercourse.

■ **APPROXIMATE TIME TO COMPLETE**

1 hour

■ **MATERIALS**

3 corks

2 or 3 rubber bands

Scissors

Construction paper

Crayons, markers, and other materials for decorating the sail

Toothpick

Tape

Straw

1. Place the three corks together and use the rubber bands to secure them in place (fig. 1).

2. Cut out a small, square piece of construction paper and draw a colorful design on both sides. Attach the sail to the toothpick with tape and stick the toothpick into the middle cork (fig. 2).

Fig. 1: Secure the corks together with two or three rubber bands.

Fig. 2: Decorate the paper sail and attach it to the cork with a toothpick.

Fig. 3: Propel your boat forward by blowing air through the straw.

3. Race your cork boat in a safe body of water, such as a swimming pool, bathtub, slow-moving creek, or a rectangular tub filled with water. To raise the difficulty level, place obstacles in the way and require each boat to sail around them. Use the straw to provide forward momentum (fig. 3).

Minecraft Play: Waterfalls and Rapids

In this part of the lab, you'll build a watery racecourse and sail your Minecraft boat through rapids and down waterfalls to victory!

■ **GAME MODE**
Build in Creative; Play in Survival

■ **APPROXIMATE TIME TO COMPLETE**
2–4 hours in Minecraft

■ **PLATFORMS**
PC/Mac, Consoles, PE

1. Determine the length of the course based on the terrain you're working with and the skill level of each builder. See the lists opposite for ideas.

2. To save construction time, consider using a natural flowing river as part of your course. Incorporate elevated and depressed land around the river to make waterfalls, rapids, and small still ponds.

 ONLINE RESOURCE
One avid builder known as TheNexusWarrior took on the challenge of telling the story of the *Titanic*, the doomed passenger liner, using Minecraft. Watch this amazing production here: *https://goo.gl/lVlqYØ*

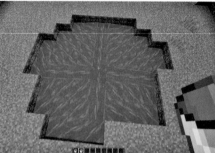

Fig. 1: To place water, line up the crosshairs and right-click with a water bucket in your hand. Have an empty bucket handy to scoop the water up again in case it isn't placed in the correct location.

3. Build a meandering course with a starting gate near your previously built parkour challenge (see Lab 18). Build it so that several players can race at the same time. The finish line can be by itself, or the course can loop back upon itself.

4. Fill the course with as many obstacles as you'd like, but don't make it so difficult that you can't complete it in a minute or two. Challenging courses include sections where the water is still and where the water is moving quickly.

Fig. 2: Signs may be used as gates to create a short-term rapid and provide a nice boost in speed.

5. These are some basic rules for working with water and boats in Minecraft:

• Water flows eight blocks on a flat space and will continue to flow as long as it is moving downhill. Boats will naturally move in that direction.

• Scoop water by right-clicking with an empty bucket at the water source. Place water by right-clicking a full water bucket (fig. 1). You cannot place water on top of water.

• Channeling water through "gates" provides a speed boost (fig. 2).

• Placing glowstone under water provides course direction at night (fig. 3).

• A fountain-like rapid effect is made by first creating and then destroying a fountain (fig. 4).

• Right-click on a boat to hop in it and left-shift to exit. Move boats in still water by pressing W, but move faster with a current.

Fig. 3: A figure eight—created here with strategically placed blocks—is always fun.

Fig. 4: To make a fountain, arrange stone blocks in the water as shown. Right-click with a water bucket on top of the tallest block. You can then destroy the blocks underneath without affecting the fountain.

MORE TO EXPLORE

Here are some other ideas for enhancing your course and the racing experience.

- Play in creative mode so players can supply their own boats.
- Automate the course by creating a redstone-powered starting gate.
- Instead of starting the race in the boat, have players run or leap to the starting line before placing their boats in the water.
- Place obstacles players must maneuver through or around. Squid make good obstacles.
- Provide opportunities for players to see and pass each other on the course.
- Create a shortcut or two, but make it challenging to reach.
- Include at least one waterfall.

Players earn bonus points by being the first to complete a section of the course.

SHARE YOUR WORK

Narrate a screencast of your race and post it on YouTube. Don't forget to add a fun soundtrack and create a colorful title for the episode. Be sure to use the hashtag *#minecrafterbook* when sharing.

To complete this quest, you'll need to connect the game elements you previously built together and have a grand, chaotic, and fun-filled race through all three. In the family activity, you'll create a blog post to share your Minecraft adventure.

Family Activity: Share the Fun

This part of the lab gives you time to reflect on the previous labs in this quest and create a blog post to share the fun with family and friends. If you haven't previously set up your family blog, refer to page 21 for advice and instructions.

■ **APPROXIMATE TIME TO COMPLETE**
1–2 hours

■ **MATERIALS**
Family blog
Screenshots of your mini games
Links to videos or to your playlist

1. You'll want everyone to contribute their experience, so take a moment to decide what each person would like to say. Younger kids might need an adult to help them express their thoughts, but older kids and adults should take turns and type their reflections on your website.

2. Don't forget to include links and add captions to your images. Gather the screenshots or links to your videos that you wish to include in your post.

3. Publish your post and share it with family and friends through your favorite social media outlets.

Minecraft Play: The Great Race

Players will be competing against each other and racing through the three mini games you've built in the previous labs in this quest. Ideally, everyone will be racing at the same time, but you may discover that it's more manageable to have players race individually against a clock. Alternatively, you can make this a team challenge where teams of two or three take turns completing one challenge and then tag their partner for the next. Whichever option you choose, set up your final challenge using the guidelines at right.

■ **GAME MODE**
Build in Creative; Play in Survival

■ **APPROXIMATE TIME TO COMPLETE**
1–2 hours in Minecraft

■ **PLATFORMS**
PC/Mac, Consoles, PE

ONLINE RESOURCE
Fireworks are a delightful addition to Minecraft. You can produce them in many different forms using many different combinations of resources. To explore firework rockets and stars, watch this short video: *https://goo.gl/GQZYIR*

Fig. 1: Design creative pathways to connect your three events.

Fig. 2: Use dyes and leather armor to create uniforms for each player or team.

1. Determine the order in which the mini games (archery tournament, parkour, and boat race) are to be completed. You do not need to complete them in the same order in which they were created.

2. Connect each mini game with creative pathways. These can be standard footpaths, or consider designing other fun ways to move between games, such as minecarts, on the back of a pig or horse, or by tiptoeing across a lava pool (fig. 1).

3. Where will the players begin the race? Create a locker room and stock it with items, armor, and dyes, which will allow players to customize their look and get their game face on (fig. 2).

4. Create a tunnel or special walkway for challengers to enter the staging area and starting point from the locker room (fig. 3).

5. Use redstone to automate the start of the race and make it a fair start for all. If you created a starting gate for your boat race (see Lab 19), begin the race there. If you want to start the race with another game, you'll need to disable the boat race's starting gate to allow racers to launch their boats as soon as they arrive.

Fig. 3: Create a special entryway for the competitors.

Fig. 4: Design the finish line so the first player to cross steps on the pressure plate connected to a dispenser and launches fireworks!

6. **Fireworks! You must create a finish line that launches fireworks when a player crosses it (fig. 4). See Online Resource (opposite page) for tips on fireworks. If your course ends with the boat race, use or modify the finish line that's already completed. If you're finishing with another game, you'll need to disable any redstone at the boat race finish line and instead guide racers to the next game.**

7. **On your marks . . . get set . . . go!**

SHARE YOUR WORK

To complete this quest, share your family blog post that reflects on the fun you had creating your mini games. Be sure to include lots of screenshots and links to the videos you created. Share your post on social media and use the hashtag *#minecrafterbook* so that others can discover your work.

MORE TO EXPLORE

This lab is a perfect place to show off your redstone skills. Pistons, tripwires, daylight sensors, dispensers, and droppers could all be used to great effect throughout this challenge, but especially in the locker room and entrance tunnel and at the starting gate and finish line.

Daylight sensors attached to lamps can provide automatic lighting on your course.

Future Thinking

QUEST 6

In this final quest, you'll use your skills from all the other quests to design and build your best work yet—a city of your own. This will be a new and improved city that is more useful and fun for its inhabitants, and it will have all the necessary features, including its own culture. What's a city without a theme park? The sky's the limit—or is it?

LAB 21

CITY PLANNING
Tour your own city with an eye on the layout and locations of features. Then plan and craft a Minecraft city with all the best parts of the city you live in.

LAB 22

CULTURE CLUB
Visit online or in person museums and other cultural landmarks. Next you'll create your own culture by crafting characters, buildings, language, and more.

LAB 23

FUN AND GAMES
Visit a theme park, then create your own in Minecraft, complete with carnival booth attractions.

LAB 24

MUSHROOM STEW
With all that building you'll be hungry. Explore deeper into your world for Mushroom Island biome to harvest mushrooms and craft a hot bowl of mushroom stew in and out of game.

City Planning

PLACE
BADGE
HERE

The ancient Incas were known for their lengthy roads connecting their cities. The Romans planned their cities and roads to efficiently house their massive populace. The city or town where you live has its own design.

In the family activity for this lab, you'll analyze the features of your city or town. Then you'll sketch out a city you'd like to build in Minecraft. Be sure to leave plenty of room for the remaining lab activities in this quest. You'll get to design the city of your dreams!

Family Activity: Take a Tour

Grab a map of your city or town, either online or on paper, then use the map to explore its features and the way it's organized.

■ **APPROXIMATE TIME TO COMPLETE**
1 hour

■ **MATERIALS**
Map of your city
Walking shoes

1. Using a map of your city, identify the different features that make your city a city. Notice the layout of different zones and the intersections of streets. Use the checklist at right to make sure you locate all its features. There are two key things you'll need to do when planning your Minecraft city: take inventory, and analyze that inventory.

2. Walk around your city, analyzing it. Walk from your house to the school, or from the library to the police station. Look at the streets and buildings. A walking tour will help you gather information as you work toward designing your ideal city in Minecraft.

3. Pick a Minecraft map for your in-game city. As with any design, you need to know about the site of your build before you can create it. If you're picking a flat map, for example, then plan anything you want; if you're planning a random-generated world, then you'll need to anticipate traveling over hills and through water.

4. Sketch out your ideal city on paper or digitally. Most cities are divided into zones or districts for business, residences, schools, industry, and agriculture.

5. Decide how far people in your city will have to travel to purchase groceries, receive help from the fire department, and get to school, among other things.

CITY PLANNING CHECKLIST
- ☐ Apartments
- ☐ Auto mechanic
- ☐ Community garden
- ☐ Courthouse and jail
- ☐ Fire department
- ☐ Grocery store
- ☐ Hospital
- ☐ Library
- ☐ Open space
- ☐ Police department
- ☐ Recreation areas (park, beach, waterslides)
- ☐ School
- ☐ Suburbs
- ☐ Tall business buildings

In the family activity, you identified the
necessary parts of a city, so now it's time
to work together to craft your ideal city.
An ideal Minecraft city will likely have
a few extra features. Consider building
your city in the sky or under water. If you
plan to play in your city in survival mode,
then you'll want to include abandoned
mineshafts and monster traps. If you
include teleport blocks, it'll be even easier
to travel from the far ends of your city.

Fig. 1: Start your build with a layout.

▩ **GAME MODE**

  Creative and Survival

▩ **APPROXIMATE TIME TO COMPLETE**

  2–3 hours in Minecraft

▩ **PLATFORMS**

  PC/Mac, Consoles, PE

1. Choose a flat world or a random seed,
   or use a map you've been working on.
   You'll need plenty of space and to-
   pography to match your ideal city. We
   created a city layout before attempting our build. The colored wool blocks
   represent zones within the city. The
   template makes it easier for others to
   help build (fig. 1).

2. Fly around your world and start the
   outline. The outline should include
   the different zones for your city. Once
   you have the outline planned inside
   of the game, switch to survival mode.
   In survival mode you'll find out how
   far each of the zones and important
   features are in your city.

Fig. 2: This garden has wildflowers and a fountain.

Fig. 3: A fancy apartment loft decorated with expensive art and a great view of the city.

MORE TO EXPLORE
Regular elevators do not exist in Minecraft. Instead, you can build an elevator shaft and pour water down from the top. The water column can double as a liquid elevator that allows you to swim up.

Fig. 4: This large office building includes cubicles for employees. All it needs are villagers to roam the halls looking busy.

3. The manner in which you build is up to your style. You may want to start with the large buildings or the important city features first, and then fill in areas with a garden (fig. 2), residences (fig. 3), and businesses (fig. 4). This is one of those builds that could be never-ending. Allow your build to evolve, as you'll want your city to change.

SHARE YOUR WORK
Share your city with other Minecraft players. Invite them to take up residence or help build out sections of the city. With the help of others, your build will become even better. Publish it online and use the hashtag *#minecrafterbook* when sharing.

Culture is the story of people. It's made up of
language, values, experiences, behaviors, art, and
architecture. Learning about culture is learning about
people. Cultures aren't always associated with race
or geography. There's a culture within Minecraft, one
that fosters curiosity, fun, discovery, exploration,
and encouragement. This lab has several examples
of different cultures as a way to inspire your own
creation. In the family activity, you'll visit cultural
spots in person or online. In-game, you'll work on
creating cultures within your city.

Family Activity: Cultural Events

Plan a trip to a cultural event, either in person or online. While at the event, take pictures and let your mind wander into the wonders of that culture. In the Minecraft section of this lab you'll get a chance to create your own culture. Find inspiration for your culture from the other cultures you experience.

▨ **APPROXIMATE TIME TO COMPLETE**
   1+ hours

▨ **MATERIALS**
   Camera
   Notepad

1. **Plan a visit to a local museum, Renaissance festival, comic con, Maker Faire, or any other cultural festival. See Online Resource at right for an alternative to actual travel.**

2. **While you visit the cultural event of your choice, take pictures and notes and make sketches. Be curious about what you see. Take time to wonder what makes that culture unique and interesting. Think about the language, food, music, and art you find there (figs. 1-3).**

Fig. 1: A village at a Renaissance fair.

Fig. 2: Dragons at a Chinese New Year festival.

Fig. 3: A Polynesian fire-knife dance.

MORE TO EXPLORE
The culture you develop for your Minecraft city can be influenced by an ancient culture. The city shown opposite was inspired by the ancient Chinese city of Chang'an and crafted by co-author John Miller and his students.

ONLINE RESOURCE
If you can't make the physical trip to a cultural event, then make your way to Google's Cultural Institute: *www.google.com/culturalinstitute*

   At the Cultural Institute, you can explore exhibits from around the world that focus on art, history, or the wonders of the world.

Minecraft Play: Craft Your Own Culture

You've researched different cultures in the family activity—now it's time to create your own culture in Minecraft. You're invited to craft a culture that you find interesting—or maybe one that's just plain silly.

■ **GAME MODE**

Creative

■ **APPROXIMATE TIME TO COMPLETE**

2–3 hours in Minecraft

■ **PLATFORMS**

PC/Mac, Consoles, PE

Fig. 1: This enchantment table doubles as a cool-looking book. This culture uses books to learn about their customs, history, and language.

ONLINE RESOURCE

Adam Clarke has an excellent video in his 101 Ideas for Minecraft Learners series on how to create a story path. You can find his video here: *https://youtu.be/uWTKlfynSuo*

1. Choose who will be in your culture. Are they monsters, villagers, or fellow players? Maybe your in-game culture is focused on the lives of zombies and other in-game monsters. Maybe you've designed your own creatures who have a language, a history, and a common set of behaviors and values. Does your culture include other players and a hierarchy among those players? What set of beliefs does your culture have? How do your people know about their history (fig. 1)?

2. If culture is a story of people, then every story has a history. Design your history and build artifacts in-game to represent that culture (fig. 2).

3. Craft the buildings appropriate to your culture. What influences are you drawing on as you craft your people? Reflect on the research from the family activity as you build buildings that reflect your version of a culture (fig. 3).

4. Don't think your culture has to follow the rules of other cultures. Add something surprising. If your culture includes monsters, perhaps your monsters are just misunderstood. Your zombies don't think they're attacking—they believe it's just a friendly way of saying hi.

Fig. 2: This chest is full of artifacts that add to this culture. On top of the chest is a small sample of the types of tools used in it.

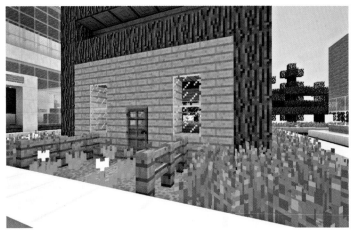

Fig. 3: The types of homes you build will affect and reflect your culture. This wooden home is plain and undecorated.

MORE TO EXPLORE

Create the story of your culture. In-game you can use command blocks to create a story. As players walk along the visual history of your culture, they activate the command blocks that tell the story through chat as well as through summoning artifacts.

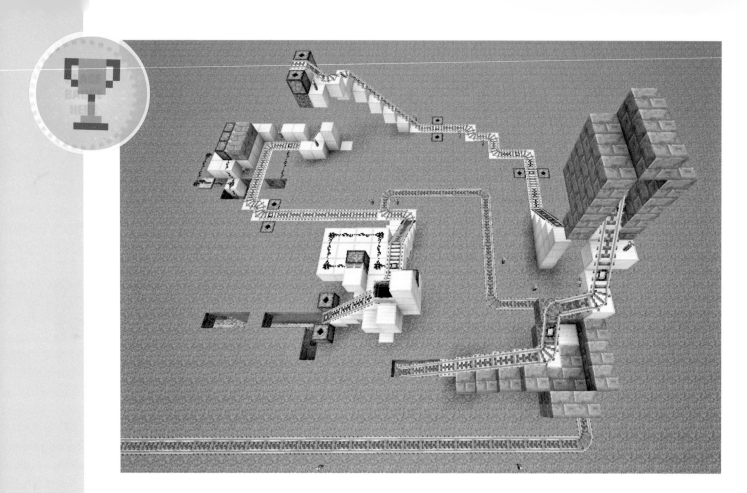

Some of the best cities have theme parks and carnivals. Whether there is a traveling carnival nearby or you are lucky enough to live close to a major theme park, you'll have an excuse to visit one in the family activity portion of this lab. In game you'll craft a theme park that fits your city and culture. Dream big.

Family Activity: Theme Park

This family activity is a great reason to purchase tickets and head off to a carnival or theme park. While there, you'll want to grab a map for later reference.

■ **APPROXIMATE TIME TO COMPLETE**
  8 hours

■ **MATERIALS**
  Tickets to a theme park or carnival
  Theme park map

1. **While visiting the theme park or researching it online, pay attention to the types of attractions and the layout of the park. Take some time to study the map (fig. 1).**

2. **Spend some time sketching your theme park. Plan from the ticketing and entrance all the way through to the rides and carnival-type booths. Do you have a rail system to make for quick transport? Which rides greet you upon entrance and which rides are all the way in the back of your park? Do you have space for parades and for onlookers to watch the fireworks?**

Fig. 1: Be sure to look at a park's map, whether you visit it in person or check it out online.

ONLINE RESOURCES
If you can't visit a carnival or theme park in person, take a look online at what several different theme parks have to offer.

MORE TO EXPLORE
It's a great conversation starter to ask your fellow Minecraft players what types of attractions theme parks should have. This will help get your imaginations flowing.

It's time to dream up some new amusement rides—in this Minecraft activity, you'll get to build them.

■ **GAME MODE**

Creative

■ **APPROXIMATE TIME TO COMPLETE**

3+ hours in Minecraft

■ **PLATFORMS**

PC/Mac, Consoles, PE

 ONLINE RESOURCES

■ There are lots of videos on theme parks in Minecraft, even one called Notchland. Notchland is a sort of theme park with Markus Persson ("Notch") as the theme.

■ If you included a maze in your theme park, be sure to check out The Maze Runner Minecraft video: *https://youtu.be/Jr3y6eegMcU*

Fig. 1: Build an archery course as part of your theme park.

1. Set aside a large chunk of your city and begin building your theme park. Create the attractions you sketched in the family activity and add on others if you like. Here's a list of fun Minecraft carnival attractions to inspire you:

• **Archery course.** Place wooden buttons as the bull's-eye that activates a redstone lamp (fig. 1)

• **Bumper boats** using a pool of water and boats (fig. 2)

• **Funhouse** with command blocks and redstone features

• **High dive.** Build a tower with a small pool of water at the bottom. Jump from the top, aiming for the pool.

• **Ice skating rink.** Add villagers to make this even sillier.

• **Maze**

• **Mini-golf course**

• **Parkour obstacle course**

• **Petting zoo**

• **Pig race with saddles**

• **Roller coaster** (fig. 3). Don't limit your coasters to what's possible in the real world. In Minecraft your coaster can even drop from one rail onto another without causing any physical damage.

• **Stationary Ferris wheel.** Although it can't move it will look at home at the park.

• **Waterslide.** Craft a tower several blocks up. From the tower build wide steps. Leave enough space at the top and bottom for a pool of water. To start your waterslide, fill the upper pool enough to overflow down the wide steps.

Fig. 2: Bumper boats are easy to make and fun to play. The first person to break his or her boat loses.

Fig. 3: No coaster is complete without the large buildup.

MORE TO EXPLORE
Build a rail around your theme park using redstone rails. Make it extra fun by building it through caves and mountains and on a beach. Install oversized creatures to spice up the ride.

2. Every theme park also has a series of booths, such as a ring toss and a milk jug throw. These are some Minecraft carnival challenge booths you may want to include in your build:

• Ring toss. Place a weighted pressure plate and toss blocks onto the pressure plate. Once enough blocks have activated the pressure plate, a piston lifts up.

• Ball bounce. Place a slime block on the ground, toss yourself on the block, and try to land in a designated area.

• Dunk tank. Have another player stand on a trapdoor. Shoot arrows at a wooden button to make the trapdoor release, making the player fall into a pool of water.

• Speed mining booth. Build a wooden wall ten blocks deep with the last block as a stone of your choice. Give each player a wooden pickaxe. The first person to collect the final block wins.

Mushroom stew is an in-game food item that's often overlooked. To complete this lab, you'll get to cook up some real stew in the family activity, then craft mushoom stew in-game.

Family Activity: Yummy Stew

Time to cook up a simple recipe of mushroom stew, or your favorite stew or soup. Your Minecraft player likely knows all about crafting in the game, so use this family activity to cook something delicious together. As you gather ingredients and prepare them for cooking, ask your Minecraft player what sort of similarities and differences there are to crafting food in the game. The process of cooking is an excellent way to connect in-game activities with real life.

■ **APPROXIMATE TIME TO COMPLETE**

1 hour

■ **INGREDIENTS**

20 small mushrooms of your choice
3 large carrots
1 onion
1 celery stalk
2 tablespoons (28 g) unsalted butter
6 cups (1420 ml) chicken stock
A pinch of fresh thyme
Salt and pepper

1. **Using the blank crafting table, draw the ingredients for the mushroom soup (fig. 1). Drawing the real-life version of the mushroom stew will help both you and your Minecraft player connect with the in-game version of crafting mushroom stew.**

2. **Chop up the mushrooms, carrots, onion, and celery (fig. 2). Place in a pot with the butter over medium heat. Cook the vegetables, stirring occasionally, until tender, 6 to 8 minutes.**

3. **Add the chicken broth and thyme. Cover and simmer for about 30 minutes, or until the vegetables are completely tender. Season to taste with salt and pepper.**

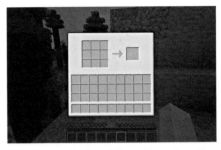

Fig. 1: Use a blank crafting table to draw the real recipe for stew or soup.

Fig. 2: Chop up the vegetables and prepare the other ingredients.

For the in-game part of the lab, you'll get to grow all the ingredients necessary to craft mushroom stew. This requires quite a bit of exploration and time. There are two different types of common mushrooms in the game, brown and red. In your exploration you may find mushrooms growing in strange places, such as on the tops of trees. See "Mushrooms in Minecraft," at right.

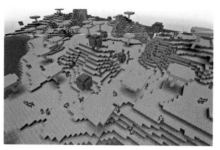

Fig. 1: Mushroom Island is a great place to collect mushrooms and mycelium blocks and watch the mysterious mooshrooms.

■ **GAME MODE**
Creative

■ **APPROXIMATE TIME TO COMPLETE**
2–3 hours in Minecraft

■ **PLATFORMS**
PC/Mac, Consoles, PE

1. Explore your world for a Mushroom Island (fig. 1).

2. Search your inventory for a shovel, anvil, and enchantment book with silk touch I. After you've placed the anvil, click the place button on the anvil. Set the shovel in the first box and the silk touch enchantment book in the second box (fig. 2). Tip: After you've enchanted the shovel with silk touch you can place it back on the anvil to rename it. Renaming your enchanted tools will help you quickly identify the one you're looking for.

3. On Mushroom Island you'll find mycelium blocks, which look like dark dirt blocks. Using your silk touch enchantment shovel, mine the mycelium blocks (fig. 3). If you use a regular shovel, the mycelium blocks become regular dirt blocks.

MUSHROOMS IN MINECRAFT

There are a couple of ways to craft mushroom stew. One is to milk mooshrooms (see page 126) with an empty bowl. Mooshrooms are a strange-looking cows that have red mushrooms growing on their backs. You can also use shears to cut off the red mushrooms while leaving the cows alive. You can use shears to collect up to five mushrooms from a mooshroom. You can also craft a bowl of the delicious stew with a brown mushroom, a red mushroom, and an empty bowl.

You can also find mushrooms in poorly lit areas, as well as in Island and Swampland biomes. They naturally spawn on Mushroom Island biomes on mycelium blocks, which look similar to dirt blocks.

In the Pocket Edition only, you can smelt a red mushroom to make rose-colored dye.

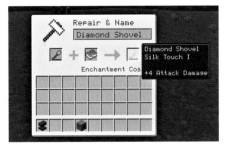
Fig. 2: Place the anvil, then set a shovel and the silk touch enchantment book to create an enchanted shovel.

Fig. 3: Mycelium blocks occur naturally on Mushroom Island. Mine lots of mycelium blocks with the enchanted silk touch shovel.

Fig. 4: Mushrooms grow best in low light. Build an underground mushroom garden using the mycelium blocks and the mushrooms you've mined.

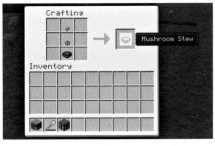
Fig. 5: Place an empty bowl on the crafting table to craft a bowl of yummy mushroom stew.

4. Dig underground to create an underground garden. Mushrooms grow best in low or no light areas. Place the mycelium blocks on the ground to provide the best chance to grow mushrooms (fig. 4). Use the ground above your mushroom farm to garden other useful crops, such as sugarcane, wheat, and melons.

5. Craft a wooden bowl. Place the empty wooden bowl and the mushrooms you grew on your crafting table (fig. 5).

MORE TO EXPLORE

- Grow huge mushrooms by placing bone meal (see page 57) on your mushrooms. Harvesting one huge mushroom can yield up to two mushrooms.

- Find and harvest a mushroom from the flower pot outside a witch hut. Look in a Swampland biome for a witch hut.

SHARE YOUR WORK

Take a picture of your mushroom stew in and outside of the game. Publish it online and use the hashtag *#minecrafterbook* when sharing.

ONLINE RESOURCES

- To save time searching for the Mushroom biome, use the Chunk Base Biome Finder: *http://goo.gl/nH3lKN*

- The Wizard Keen in Stampy's show *Wonder Quest* can often be caught eating mushroom stew. Sometimes a mushroom will be left in his beard!

Extras

SCAVENGER HUNT
CHECKLIST

- ☐ Apple
- ☐ Bed
- ☐ Boat
- ☐ Bow and arrow
- ☐ Bread
- ☐ Cactus
- ☐ Cake
- ☐ Carpet
- ☐ Carrot
- ☐ Coal or charcoal
- ☐ Cobweb
- ☐ Compass
- ☐ Clay
- ☐ Diamond
- ☐ Dirt
- ☐ Egg
- ☐ Emerald
- ☐ Fish
- ☐ Fishing rod

- ☐ Flower pot
- ☐ Flowers
- ☐ Furnace
- ☐ Gold
- ☐ Glass
- ☐ Grass
- ☐ Gravel
- ☐ Hoe
- ☐ Ice or snow
- ☐ Iron
- ☐ Ladder
- ☐ Leather
- ☐ Leaves
- ☐ Melon
- ☐ Milk
- ☐ Music disc
- ☐ Obsidian
- ☐ Painting
- ☐ Pickaxe

- ☐ Pumpkin pie
- ☐ Saddle
- ☐ Sand
- ☐ Shovel
- ☐ Sign
- ☐ Spider eye
- ☐ Sponge
- ☐ Stairs
- ☐ Sticks
- ☐ Stone
- ☐ String
- ☐ Sugar
- ☐ Tree
- ☐ Vines
- ☐ Water bottle
- ☐ Water bucket
- ☐ Wheat
- ☐ Wood plank
- ☐ Wool

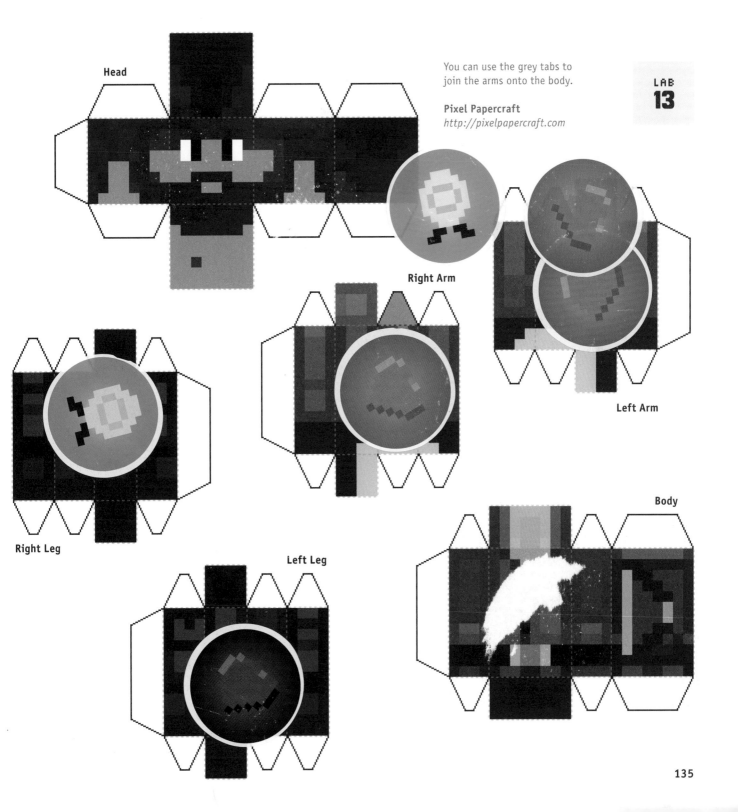

Head

You can use the grey tabs to join the arms onto the body.

Pixel Papercraft
http://pixelpapercraft.com

Right Arm

Left Arm

Right Leg

Left Leg

Body

LABS
12, 13
16, 18

Resources

123d Circuits
www.123dapp.com/circuits

3D Printing
printcraft.org

Adam Clarke YouTube Channel
youtube.com/user/adamgorgeous

Adobe Captivate
www.adobe.com/products/captivate.html

All Recipes
www.allrecipes.com

Blockworks
blockworksmc.com

Bow and Arrow Toy
http://goo.gl/P4Tor

Camtasia
www.techsmith.com/camtasia.html

Chunk Base Biome Finder
http://goo.gl/nH3lKN

Creative Commons Music
http://creativecommons.org/ legalmusicforvideos

Egg Farming
http://goo.gl/O8Øo6h

Food.
www.food.com

Firework Rockets
https://goo.gl/GQZYIR

FyreUK
https://goo.gl/C1BYQc

Google Cultural Institute
www.google.com/culturalinstitute

Hot Potato Game
http://goo.gl/FeTnBQ

Jesper the End's Minecraft Disco Party
https://youtu.be/MLAoVwR4d8Ø

John Miller's Blog
http://minecraft.edtecworks.com

Making of *When Stampy Came to Tea*
https://goo.gl/2PYeKp

Maze Runner in Minecraft
https://youtu.be/Jr3y6eegMcU

Minecraft Wiki
minecraft.gamepedia.com

Note Blocks, Advanced
https://goo.gl/1pYPsh

Note Blocks, Popular Songs
https://goo.gl/OTj5m8

Parkour Race
https://goo.gl/s9Ptaa

Pixel Art
http://goo.gl/gCPbOE

PixelPaperCraft
pixelpapercraft.com

Round Objects in Minecraft
www.plotz.co.uk

Screencast-O-Matic
www.screencast-o-matic.com

Shadow Puppets
https://goo.gl/4RVGhI

Story Path by Adam Clarke
https://youtu.be/uWTKlfynSuo

Tate Modern Museum Minecraft Worlds
http://goo.gl/Nvg2DB

TheKitchn
www.thekitchn.com

The *Titanic*
https://goo.gl/lVlqYØ

TNT Cannon by DanTDM
https://goo.gl/4Haq7A

Traps, Advanced Building Techniques
http://goo.gl/ZVX7mu

When Stampy Came to Tea
https://goo.gl/BEssTn

YouTube Editor
youtube.com/editor

Zombie Party YouTube Playlist
https://goo.gl/nHMWpY

ACKNOWLEDGMENTS

Foremost, we would like to thank our families and express our deepest gratitude for their support and assistance throughout the process of writing this book. Without their love, creative ideas, and enthusiastic assistance, this book would not be what it is.

About the Authors

JOHN MILLER lives in Paso Robles, California, and holds multiple and single-subject credentials in history and science. He has been a middle school teacher for more than twenty years and has taught every subject in grades 6 through 8. He also holds a master's degree in educational technology and instructional design from San Diego State University and is a Google for Education Certified Innovator, a San Luis Obispo County CUE board president, and a CUE Lead Learner. John is a featured presenter at conferences and workshops around the country. He loves teaching twenty-first-century skills to his students and his passions include student blogging, e-learning, Minecraft in the classroom, photography, Apple, and Google. John is a contributor to *Minecraft in the Classroom* (Peachpit Press, 2014).

CHRIS FORNELL SCOTT is the father of three Minecraft-loving boys. He and his wife love to see their enthusiasm as they play cooperatively. The game has some magic power to transform brothers into creative collaborators. He is an authorized Google for Education Certified Trainer and Innovator, a Santa Barbara CUE board member, and CUE Lead Learner. Chris works to design the classroom culture and environment. He and co-author John Miller started MinecrafterCamp.com as a way to help kids and teachers learn how to squeeze the learning power out of Minecraft. Chris loves using design thinking, an agile project management process in the classroom, and enjoys seeing his students enter the flow of learning. He loves to help others in their educational journey. You'll find Chris at conferences around the world presenting on classroom culture, technology, and design. He's giddy with excitement to use this book with his own kids. Like most homes, the Scott house struggles with balancing screen time, and this book is his solution.

Index

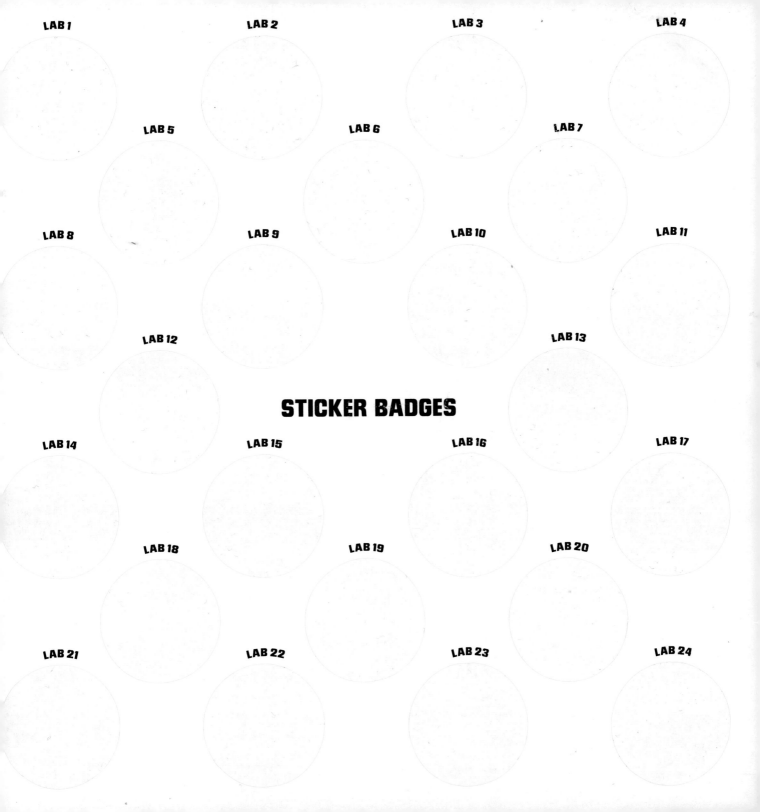

LAB 1

LAB 2

LAB 3

LAB 4

LAB 5

LAB 6

LAB 7

LAB 8

LAB 9

LAB 10

LAB 11

LAB 12

LAB 13

STICKER BADGES

LAB 14

LAB 15

LAB 16

LAB 17

LAB 18

LAB 19

LAB 20

LAB 21

LAB 22

LAB 23

LAB 24